UPANIṢADS

Upaniṣads

(*Selections from 108 Upaniṣads*)

T.M.P. Mahadevan

MOTILAL BANARSIDASS PUBLISHERS
PRIVATE LIMITED • DELHI

First Published: Delhi, 1975
Reprint: Delhi, 1999, 2000, **2010**

ISBN: 81-208-1611-0

Also available at:

MOTILAL BANARSIDASS

236, 9th Main III Block, Jayanagar, Bangalore 560 011
41 U.A. Bungalow Road, Jawahar Nagar, Delhi 110 007
8 Mahalaxmi Chamber, Warden Road, Mumbai 400 026
120 Royapettah High Road, Mylapore, Chennai 600 004
Sanas Plaza, 1302 Baji Rao Road, Pune 411 002
8 Camac Street, Calcutta 700 017
Ashok Rajpath, Patna 800 004
Chowk, Varanasi 221 001

Printed in India

BY JAINENDRA PRAKASH JAIN AT SHRI JAINENDRA PRESS,
A-45 NARAINA, PHASE-I, NEW DELHI 110 028
AND PUBLISHED BY NARENDRA PRAKASH JAIN FOR
MOTILAL BANARSIDASS PUBLISHERS PRIVATE LIMITED,
BUNGALOW ROAD, DELHI 110 007

CONTENTS

INTRODUCTION

1. NATURE AND SCOPE OF THE UPANIṢADS

The *Upaniṣads* constitute the concluding portions of the *Vedas*. They are the summits of early Indian thought, and have been aptly described as the 'Himalayas of the Soul.'[1] To vary the metaphor, the *Upaniṣads* form the basic springs of Indian philosophy; and they provide the inspiration not only for the orthodox systems but also for the so-called heterodox schools. Everytime there was a renaissance in India, the call of the leaders, in essence, has been : "Back to the *Upaniṣads* !" Every reformer and captain of thought has striven to recapture the spirit of these immortal texts. Speaking, for instance, of the opening passage of the first of the *Upaniṣads*, *Mahātmā* Gandhi once said : "I have now come to the final conclusion that if all the *Upaniṣads* and all the other scriptures happened all of a sudden to be reduced to ashes and if only the first verse in the *Īśopaniṣad* were left intact in the memory of the Hindus, Hinduism would live for ever."[2]

Everyone who has had a genuine acquaintance with the *Upaniṣads* has showered on them unstinted praise. Schopenhauer who read the

Latin translation of a Persian rendering of the *Upaniṣads* felt so exalted by the thoughts found therein that he always had a copy of it on his table, and "was in the habit, before going to bed, of performing his devotions from its pages." His words of adoration have been often quoted and will bear repetition. "That incomparable book," he says, "stirs the spirit to the very depths of the soul. From every sentence deep, original and sublime thoughts arise, and the whole is pervaded by a high and holy and earnest spirit . . . In the whole world there is no study, except that of the originals, so beneficial and so elevating as that of the Oupnekhat (i.e. *Upaniṣad*). It has been the solace of my life, and it will be the solace of my death."[3] In almost identical terms, Paul Deussen speaks of the philosophy of the *Upaniṣads* as "the strongest support of pure morality, the greatest consolation in the sufferings of life and death."[4] To quote only one other Orientalist, Max Müller, the *Upaniṣads* are to him "like the light of the morning, like the pure air of the mountains—so simple, so true, if once understood."[5]

The secret of the charm of the *Upaniṣads* lies both in the philosophy of spiritual monism or non-dualism which they teach and the manner in which this teaching is given. Reality is declared to be non-dual, one without a second; and this Reality is identified with Spirit or Self higher than which there is nothing. Not only is the non-duality of Self affirmed, but also the plurality of things is declared to be ultimately not real. "From death to death he goes who sees plurality here as it were."[6] There is something fascinating about this non-duality philosophy. As William James was forced to admit, "*An Absolute One, and I that One*, . . . surely we have here a religion which, emotionally considered, has a high pragmatic value."[7] This is, of course, the least that can be said of the Upaniṣadic monism.

The *Upaniṣads* are not systematic treatises on philosophy; they are not the works of any single author. The sages whose intuitions are recorded in the *Upaniṣads* are more mystic seers than mere investigators of metaphysics. There is a directness about their teachings, and an authenticity born of first-hand experience in the highest reality. They pour forth their findings in the form of stories and parables, informal discussions and intimate dialogues. The method they adopt is "more poetic than philosophic". Even where the language used is prose, the poetic quality is only too evident. It is true that in many places symbolic expressions are employed which hide the meaning rather than make it patent. Sometimes there are puns on words and mystic explanations of certain abstruse terms. Even these, it may be noted, add to the charm of the *Upaniṣads*. Charles Johnston compares these books of wisdom to "the deep, still mountain tarns, fed from the pure water of the everlasting snows,lit by clear sunshine, or, by night, mirroring the high serenity of the stars;" and he finds in them, "besides high intuition, a quaint and delightful flavour, a charm of child-like simplicity; yet of a child who is older than all age, a child of the eternal and the infinite, whose simplicity is better than the wisdom of the wise."[8]

Upaniṣads, as we have noted, form the concluding portions of the *Veda.* So they are called *Vedānta* (*Veda* + *anta;* end of *Veda*). The expression is significant also in the sense that the teaching of the *Upaniṣads* represents the aim or goal of the *Veda.* The Sanskrit word *anta*, like the English *and*, may be used to mean both "terminus" and "aim". The later Vedāntic schools derive their name from the fact that they claim to interpret the *Upaniṣads.* The etymological meaning of the term "*Upaniṣad*" is "to sit (*sad*) close by (*upa*) devotedly (*ni*)", and is indicative of the manner in which the doctrines embodied in the *Upaniṣads* were learnt at first by pupils in small conclaves sitting near their respective teachers. The expression which thus means "a session" came to be applied in course of time to what was taught at such sessions. As the *Upaniṣads* are regarded as teaching the highest truth, they could be imparted only to those who were competent to receive and benefit by them; and such competent pupils could be only a few at any given time. So, the meaning "secret" came to be attached to the term "*Upaniṣads*"; and it is in this sense that we find the expression used in the *Upaniṣads* themselves. When, for instance, some important formula is given in the *Upaniṣads*, it is characterized as the *Upaniṣad*. Thus in the *Bṛhadāraṇyaka*, the formula "The Real of the real" *(satyasya satyam)* is described as the *Upaniṣad* of the universal Soul. We come across also such expressions as "the secret teaching" *(guhya ādeśaḥ)*, "the supreme secret" *(paramaṁ guhyam)* applied to what may be considered to be the key-passages in the *Upaniṣads*. Commentators like Śaṅkara interpret the expression "*Upaniṣad*" to mean what "destroys" ignorance or what "leads" to Brahman, a meaning which correctly defines the scope and aim of the *Upaniṣads*.

The texts that bear the name '*Upaniṣad*' are now known to be more than two hundred. One of the *Upaniṣads*, *Muktikā*, gives the names of one hundred and eight *Upaniṣads*. Many of these texts, however, are late compositions, distant imitations of the ancient canonical *Upaniṣads*. One of the criteria by which the canonical nature of an *Upaniṣad* may be judged is by asking the question whether it has been commented upon or is quoted from by a thinker like Śaṅkara. Judged by this test, the first ten *Upaniṣads* mentioned in the *Muktikā* along with a few from the rest may be regarded as ancient and genuine. They are : *Īśāvāsya*, *Kena*, *Kaṭha*, *Praśna*, *Muṇḍaka*, *Māṇḍūkya*, *Taittirīya*, *Aitareya*, *Chāndogya*, *Bṛhadāraṇyaka*, *Kauṣītakī*, *Maitrāyaṇīya* and *Śvetāśvatara*. Even of these, the *Bṛhadāraṇyaka* and the *Chāndogya* are the most important, as they are not only old and comprehensive texts, but also represent the two main traditions of thought in the *Upaniṣads*, the acosmic *(niṣprapañca)* and the cosmic *(saprapañca)* respectively.

2. TWO KINDS OF KNOWLEDGE

The *Upaniṣads* make a distinction between two kinds of knowledge, the higher *(para)* and the lower *(apara)*. The lower knowledge consists of all the empirical sciences and arts as also of such sacred knowledge as relates to things and enjoyments that perish. It is interesting to note that even the four *Vedas* are included in the category of lower knowledge. A great scholar, Nārada, in spite of his encyclopaedic learning, both secular and sacred, finds that he is sorrow-stricken, and so seeks enlightenment from a sage, Sanatkumāra. The sage asks Nārada to state his credentials. Nārada reels off a long list of the arts and the sciences which he had mastered. The sage characterizes the knowledge that is represented by all these disciplines as mere name (*nāma eva*), and declares that that alone is the supreme knowledge which relates to the Imperishable (*akṣara*). This higher knowledge is described as that whereby what had not been heard of becomes heard of, what has not been thought of becomes thought of, what has not been understood becomes understood. This is further explained as the knowledge of the ground which is more than and inclusive of the knowledge of the various expressions or manifestations of the ground. "Just as by one piece of clay all that is made of clay may be known . . . the modification being only a name depending on a word; the truth being that it is just clay . . . so is that teaching.'"[9] Compared with the knowledge of the ultimate ground which is the absolute Self, the lower knowledge is nescience or false knowledge *(avidyā)*. "Widely contrasted and different are these two," says the *Kaṭha-upaniṣad*, "nescience (*avidyā*) and what is known as knowledge (*vidyā*).'"[10] The *Śvetāśvatara* refers to knowledge and ignorance that are placed hidden in the imperishable, infinite, supreme *Brahman*, and characterizes ignorance as a thing perishable and knowledge as a thing immortal.[11]

The supreme wisdom, then, is knowledge of the Self. But this knowledge is not to be confused with what we ordinarily refer to as knowledge. In this sense, it may be said that the Self is unknowable. How, then, can one speak intelligibly of Self-knowledge ? The most prominent sage in the *Bṛhadāraṇyaka-upaniṣad*, Yājña-valkya, teaches the significance of the term *knowledge* with reference to the Self thus : "Where there is duality, as it were, there one sees another, one smells another, one hears another, one thinks of another, one understands another. Where, however, everything has become just one's own self, there whereby and whom would one smell, see, hear, speak to, think of, or understand ?"[12] This, then, is the answer to the question about the unknowability of the self. The self is unknowable, not because it is unknown, but because it is the basis of all knowledge, nay, knowledge *per se.* In short, it cannot be known as objects are known. "You cannot see the seer of seeing. You cannot hear the hearer of hearing. You cannot think the thinker of thinking. You cannot understand the understander of understanding. He is your soul, which is in all things."[13] The *Kena-upaniṣad* teaches the same doctrine when it says that thither, i.e., to the self, the eye goes not, nor speech nor mind, and that it is other than the known and above the unknown.[14] The *Taittirīya-upaniṣad* declares that words and mind turn back, not being able to attain it.[15] Our words and thoughts are adequate only to the realm of plurality; they fail with reference to the non-dual Spirit. Yet, we have to make use of them as indicators or sign-posts, and not as vehicles taking us to the very end. "As a unity the self is to be looked upon . . . this unknowable, constant Being, free from blemishes, beyond space, the unborn self, great, permanent."[16] The self is to be comprehended as "It is".[17] This is the supreme knowledge, *parā vidyā,* true wisdom. The *Upaniṣads* ask us to seek this knowledge from a competent teacher who is not only learned but also in possession of the plenary experience. It is true that such a teacher is difficult to get; but so is a competent pupil. All good things are rare and hard to accomplish. "Wonderful is the declarer, proficient the obtainer of Him! Wonderful the knower, proficiently taught!"[18]

3. BRAHMAN-ĀTMAN

The supreme knowledge, as we have seen, is knowledge of the Self, which is referred to in the *Upaniṣads* as *Brahman* and *Ātman.* These two words are central to the Upaniṣadic philosophy, and their meaning, therefore, should be rightly understood. The world "*Brahman*" probably meant at first "prayer" or "speech", from the root *bṛh*, "to burst forth" or "to grow". Eventually, it came to signify the ground of the universe or the source of all existence, that which has burst forth into the universe, or that from which the universe has grown. The other word "*Ātman*" might have meant "breath", but, then, it soon came to be the expression for the soul or self of living being, especially of man. And, the remarkable discovery which the Upaniṣadic sages made was that the two are one and same : the *Ātman* is *Brahman*. This doctrine of unity is the greatest contribution which the *Upaniṣads* have made to the thought of the world. As Deussen says, "It will be found to possess a significance reaching far beyond the *Upaniṣads*, their time and country : nay, we claim for it an inestimable value for the whole race of mankind."[19]

The two terms "*Brahman*" and "*Ātman*" are used as synonyms in the *Upaniṣads*. The *Chāndogya-upaniṣad*, for instance, frames the central metaphysical question thus : "Which is the *Ātman ?* What is *Brahman ?*"[20] Here, obviously, *Ātman* and *Brahman* appear as interchangeable terms. In some contexts where the inquiry is into the source of the universe, the expression "*Ātman*" is employed, and in some other contexts where the topic discussed is the true self of man the term "*Brahman*" is used. In the *Chāndogya-upaniṣad*, a king, while describing the Reality which is the source of the universe, refers to it as the cosmic *Ātman*. In the *Taittirīya-upaniṣad*, a young seeker, Bhṛgu, makes an analysis of the sheaths that cover the self, while the term of reference is *Brahman*. Thus, to the *Upaniṣads*, *Brahman* and *Ātman* mean the same Reality. That which is without is identical with that which is within. Through the inquiry into the source of the universe and through the quest after the true self, the discovery was made that it is the one non-dual Reality that appears as the manifold world and as the plurality of individual souls. This result was rendered possible because of the unique method of the *Upaniṣads* which is a synthesis of the objective and the subjective ways of approach to Reality.

The quest is the same whether the aim is to find out the ground of the universe, or to determine the true nature of the Self. The technique of pursuing the quest is also the same : one has to go from the grosser manifestations to the subtler ones. The *Upaniṣads* are replete with illustrations which exploit this technique and exhibit the truth of non-duality. Let us look at a few cases :

(1) In the philosophical contest that was held at the court of king Janaka, Gārgī, a woman-sage, questions Yājñavalkya about the support of all things. The precise form in which the question is put is "On what is all this woven, warp and woof ?" In a series of answers, Yājñavalkya leads the inquirer to higher and higher worlds; and lastly, when the lady asks him, on what is space woven, warp and woof he replies that it is the Imperishable

(akṣara) which is the support of space. Another questioner, Uddālaka, enquires about the inner controller of all things. In a set of beautiful passages, Yājñavalkya explains that the principle that lies behind all things, cosmic as well as individual, the principle which these things do not know but which controls them from within, is the inner ruler; and this ruler, says Yājñavalkya addressing Uddālaka, is your own immortal self. "He who dwelling in all things, yet is other than all things, whom all things do not know, whose body all things are, who controls all things from within . . . He is your self, the inner ruler, immortal."[21]

(2) Bhṛgu approaches his father Varuṇa with the request for instruction about the nature of *Brahman*. Varuṇa gives his son a formula which is indicative of the general nature of reality, and asks him to discover for himself the truth through austere inquiry (*tapas*). "That, verily, whence these beings are born, that by which when born they live, that into which on departing they enter—that be desirous of knowing. That is *Brahman*."[22] Bhṛgu makes of this formula the base of his operations and enters upon the quest after the real. The first discovery that he makes is that food (*anna*, i.e. matter) is essential for existence. But soon he realizes that food is only the outer shell of what animates it, i.e. life *(prāṇa)*. Even this knowledge does not satisfy him; for upon

further inquiry he finds that mind *(manas)* is the substratum of life. Subsequent analysis reveals to Bhṛgu that mind too is a product and cannot answer to the definition of *Brahman* given by his father. He now thinks that intellectual awareness *(vijñāna)* is the final reality. Just as materialism, vitalism, and mentalism were found wanting on closer scrutiny, intellectualism too is seen to be inadequate. And at last, Bhṛgu arrives at the final truth that Bliss *(ānanda)* is *Brahman*. In this delight which is the Absolute there is no distinction of the enjoyer and the object enjoyed. In the Infinite there is no division.

(3) The Indra-Virocana myth related in the *Chāndogya* is illustrative of the fact that both competence and persistent inquiry are required for understanding the nature of the self. Prajāpati, the lord of creatures, said, "The self which is free from sin, free from old age, free from death and sorrow, hunger and thirst, whose desire is the real, whose conception is the real—that should be sought, that one should be sought, that one should desire to know."[23] The gods *(devas)* and the demons *(asuras)* heard this, and they desired to know more about the self. Indra, the sovereign of the gods, and Virocana, the chief of the demons, were sent as envoys on the mission of learning from Prajāpati knowledge of the Self. The two approached

Prajāpati, dwelt with him for thirty-two years as his pupils, and then asked him about the self. Prajāpati said to them : "The Person that is seen in the eye, that is the self. That is the immortal, the fearless. That is *Brahman.*" The implication of this teaching is that the principle responsible for seeing and knowledge is self. But the pupils misunderstood Prajāpati's teaching. They thought that the image of a person which is seen formed in the eye of the one who sees is the self. The corollary they drew was that the reflection of the body that is observed in media like water and mirror is the self. When they conveyed this inference of theirs to Prajāpati, he simply said, "Look at yourselves in a pan of water, and whatever you do not understand of the self, tell me." Indra and Virocana looked at their own reflections in water, and reported to their teacher that they saw themselves in the water "to the very hairs and nails". Prajāpati asked them to look again in a pan of water after adorning themselves, putting on their best clothes and cleaning themselves. They did as they were told, and perfectly satisfied with their fine reflections, went away thinking that the reflection and the body that was reflected constituted the self. Prajāpati did not correct them at that stage, for he wanted to test their competence and give the true doctrine only to him that had proved his fitness. Virocana returned to his clan and spread among the demons the philosophy which he thought he had learnt. "The body is the self," he said, "it alone is to be worshipped; it alone is to be served." Though at first this doctrine seemed to satisfy Indra, very soon he discovered a serious defect in it. When the body is well adorned, dressed and cleaned, the reflection appears well adorned, dressed and cleaned. But how would the reflection be if the body were blind, lame or crippled ? It too would certainly be blind, lame or crippled. And if that were the self, it would perish when the body perished. Indra saw no good in such a doctrine. Without returning to his tribe, he went back to Prajāpati and expressed to him his difficulty. After a second period of studentship for thirty-two years, Indra was led a step higher. Prajāpati now said to him, "He who moves about happy in a dream—he is the self. That is immortal, the fearless. That is *Brahman*." Indra pondered over the implications of this new teaching. It is true that the self of the dream-state is not affected by the defects of the physical body. Yet it is not all happiness that is experienced in dreams. There are also bad dreams and nightmares in which the self appears afflicted, is chased, becomes conscious of pain, and weeps. So, for the third time Indra went to Prajāpati; and at the end of a further period of apprenticeship for thirty-two years, he was instructed by Prajāpati thus : "When one is sound asleep, composed, restful, and sees no dream, that is the self. That is the immortal, the fearless. That is *Brahman*." In sleep the self is not afflicted, there is no sorrow. But, reflected Indra, there is ignorance, annihilation of consciousness as it were, in so far as one does not know oneself. So, he returned to his teacher once more for further light on his problem. This time he had to wait only for five years, at the end of which period Prajāpati gave him the final doctrine. What the teacher said was that the self should be distinguished from the body which is its temporary abode, and the various states of experience. So long as one identifies oneself with the body, one is tossed between pleasure and pain.. When one is freed from this wrong identification, there is for him neither pleasure nor pain. When the true knowledge is gained, the self realizes its nature as bliss and consciousness. Indra received this doctrine and carried it to the gods.

(4) In the *Māṇḍūkya-upaniṣad* we have a lucid analysis of the three states of experience : waking, dream, and deep sleep. The *Upaniṣad* begins by identifying the mystic sound *Om* with all-that-which-is. *Om* is all this—what was, what is, and what will be. It is also what is beyond the three divisions of time, i.e., the

unmanifest ground of the manifest universe. All this is *Brahman*, of which *Om* is the sound-symbol. The self is *Brahman*. Then, our text goes on to show how corresponding to the three modes (*mātrās*) of *Om* (*a u m*) and the fourth modeless (*amātra*) part there are the three forms in which the self appears in the states of waking, dream and sleep respectively, and the fourth which is the natural estate of the self, the unchanging and unconditioned *Turīya*. In the state of waking, the self consorts with the objects of sense which are external, and its enjoyments are gross. In dreams it revels in a world of images, and its experience is subtle. In sleep there are no desires, nor dreams; the self becomes one, without the distinction of seer and seen object; it remains then as a mass sentience, as bliss enjoying bliss. The self of the three states is designated respectively as *Vaiśvānara, Taijsasa* and *Prājña*. The fourth, *caturtha* (or *turīya*), which is the real self is beyond the changing modes of existence. It is not caught in the triple stream of waking, dream and sleep, though it is the underlying substrate of these states. It is invisible; it is not the content of empirical usage; it cannot be grasped, it does not have identifying marks; it is unthinkable and unnamable, it is the one self which is the essence of consciousness; it is that into which the universe gets resolved; it is tranquil bliss which is non-dual. Thus does the *Māṇḍūkya* teach the real nature of the self.

(5) The ultimate reality, according to the *Upaniṣads*, is not a subject set over against objects, nor an object, a *being* there ; it is that which underlies both subject and object, and transcends them. This truth could be realized only when the apparent distinction between the cosmic and the individual forms of the self is discarded, when the identity between *Brahman* and *Ātman* is recognized. In the *Chāndogya* we find this teaching of identity given in an elaborate manner to Śvetaketu by his father Uddālaka. After twelve years of study under a teacher, Śvetaketu returns home, conceited, thinking himself learned, proud. Uddālaka notices this, and at once concludes that his son has not received the only true knowledge that is worth having, i.e. the knowledge of ultimate reality. He thereupon undertakes to teach his son and thus complete his education. He begins with a description of the Being (*sat*) which alone was in the beginning, one only, without a second. It thought, "May I become many !" From it fire came into being; from fire water was born; and from water food. These three are the rudiments of the universe. Having created them, the *sat* entered into them and manifested names and forms (*nāma-rūpa*) by a process of

triplication (*trivṛtkaraṇa*), i. e. by mixing tbe three elements, fire, water and food, in different proportions. All things and beings are made of these elements, including mind, breath and speech. In sleep all these are resolved, and one returns to the *sat*, the real self, one becomes one's self. The *sat* is the root of all creatures ; they have the *sat* as their home and support. Having shown in this way that the one reality is the ground of all existence and the source of all being, Uddālaka, "suddenly and with a dramatic swiftness of transformation" identifies this reality with the self of Śvetaketu. "That which is the finest essence—this whole world has that as its soul. That is reality. That is the *Ātman*. That thou art, O Śvetaketu !"[24] This declaration of non-difference is repeated nine times, thereby indicating that it constitutes the central teaching of Uddālaka. It must be noted, however, that it is not the individual soul that is stated here to be the ground of all being. The philosophy of the *Upaniṣads* is not a variety of subjective idealism. It is true that the individual soul is non-different from the universal Spirit. But it is the universal Spirit that explains the whole world and the individual souls as individuals.

4. COSMIC AND ACOSMIC MODES

The *Upaniṣads* conceive of *Brahman-Ātman* in two modes : (i) as the all-inclusive ground of the universe, and (ii) as the reality of which the universe is but an appearance. The former is the cosmic view (*saprapañca*) of the Absolute, while the latter is the acosmic view (*niṣprapañca*). It is the difference between these two views that made possible divergence later on between the theistic and the absolutistic schools of Vedānta. We shall illustrate the two stand-points by citing a few texts from the *Upaniṣads*. The cosmic view of reality may be discerned in the following passages : "He who consists of mind, whose body is life, whose form is light, whose conception is truth, whose soul is space, containing all works, all desires, all odours and all tastes, encompassing the whole world, the speechless and the calm—this soul of mine within the heart is smaller than a grain of rice, or a barley-corn, or a mustard-seed, or a grain of millet, or the kernel of a grain of millet ; this soul of mine within the heart is greater than the earth, greater than the mid-region, greater than heaven, greater than all these worlds."[25] "The self, indeed, is below. The self is above. The self is to the west. The self is to the east. The self is to the south. The self is to the north. The self, indeed, is this whole world."[26] "He is Brahmā ; he is Indra ; he is Prajāpati ; he is all these gods ; and these five great elements, namely earth, air, ether, water, and fire ; these things and those which are mingled of the fine, as it were ; seeds of one sort or another ; those born from eggs, those born from wombs, those born from sweat, and those born from sprouts ; horses, cattle, men, elephants ; whatever creature there is here whether moving or flying, and what is stationary."[27] As typical of the texts that teach the acosmic view, the following may be considered : "This is imperishable, O Gārgī, which the wise men adore—not gross, not subtle, not short, not long, not red, not adhesive, without shadow, without darkness, without air, without space, without attachment, without taste, without smell, without eyes, without ears, without speech, without mind, without light, without breath, without mouth, without measure, and without either inside or outside. Not that does anything eat, nor that does eat anything."[28] "Devoid of sound, of touch, of form, without decay, and likewise devoid of taste, eternal, and devoid of odour, beginningless, endless, superior to the Great (*Mahat*) and firm ; realizing that, one is released from the jaws of death."[29]

The negative description of *Brahman-Ātman* should not be taken to mean that the ultimate reality is a blank, a mere nothing. It only signifies that the Absolute cannot be delimited by the categories known to human thought. In order to understand the implications of the negative texts, one must construe them along with other texts which are positive in form—the texts, for instance, which refer to *Brahman* as existence (*sat*), consciousness (*cit*), and bliss (*ānanda*). These expressions, it is true, are not to be understood in their ordinary signification. But they represent the highest concepts the mind of man has been able to evolve to indicate the nature of the supreme Spirit. The *Bṛhadāraṇyaka* describes *Brahman* as "the Real of the real" (*satyasya satyam*);[30] and splitting the word *satyam* into three syllables, *sa-ti-yam*, the *Upaniṣad* says that the first syllable and the third mean truth, while the second syllable signifies untruth, and that the whole word implies the enclosement of untruth on both sides by truth. That the self is consciousness (*caitanya*) is declared in several texts. One of the modes in which this is taught is to say that the self is the light of all lights, that it is self-luminous. "Not there does the sun shine, nor the moon and the stars ; nor do these lightnings shine, much less this fire. After Him, as He shines, does everything shine ; by His lustre is the whole world illumined."[31] *Brahman* is not only unconditioned existence and self-luminous intelligence, but also unexcellable bliss (*ānanda*). In the *Bṛhadāraṇyaka* and the *Taittirīya*, a calculus of bliss is given, taking the highest human bliss as the unit measure. According to the former *Upaniṣad*, the bliss that is

Brahman is a billion times that of the human bliss ; and according to the latter, it is a hundred trillion times superior to the highest bliss of man. The implication of such teaching is that *Brahman*-bl'ss is unlimited and measureless. The *Chāndogya* describes *Brahman* as the infinite (*bhūman*) which alone is bliss (*sukham*), and declares that there is no bliss in the small (*alpa*). In later Vedāntic literature, *Brahman* is referred to as *sac-cid-ānanda*, a formula coined out of the texts such as the ones we have considered. The *Bṛhadāraṇyaka* defines *Bṛahman* as consciousness and bliss (*vijñānam ānandam brahma*).[32] The *Taittirīya* says, "*Braman* is reality, consciousness and infinitude (*satyam jñānam anantam brahma*)."[33]

5. WORLD-EVOLUTION AND WORLD APPEARANCE

Even as there are two modes of envisaging the nature of *Brahman*, there are two standpoints from which the world may be viewed. The two views are : (i) that the world is an emanation from *Brahman*, and (ii) that it is an appearance of *Brahman*. These views came to be referred to later on as the theory of transformation (*pariṇāmavāda)*, and the theory of transfiguration (*vivarta-vāda)*, respectively. But, whether the world is a modification or an appearance, the ground thereof, according to the

Upaniṣads, it must be noted, is *Brahman*. The source of thc universe is not a category of matter, but the supreme Spirit. The *Śvetāśvatara* begins with such questions as "What is the cause? whence are we born? Whereby do we live? On what are we established? And by whom supervised do we experience our pains and pleasures ?" It finds that an adequate answer to these questions cannot be given in terms of any material or finite principle. Time *(kāla)*, nature (Svabhāva), necessity (*niyati*), chance (*yadṛcchā*), the elements (*bhūta*), the womb (*yoni*) or the male (*puruṣa*) cannot serve as the first cause. The *Upaniṣad* discovers that over all these, which may be regarded only as the secondary causes, there rules the self-power (*ātmaśakti*) of God (*deva*), hidden in His own qualities (*guṇa*). A second point on which most of the creation-texts of the *Upaniṣads* are agreed is that Brahman does not create the universe out of an extraneous matter, but that the universe is a manifestation of an aspect of *Brahman*. *Brahman* is immanent as well as transcendent. In the terminology of later Vedānta, it is the material as also the efficient cause of the world (*abhinna-nimitto'pādāna-kāraṇa*). In the *Chāndogya* text "All this, verily, is *Brahman*. Tranquil, let one worship it as *tajjalān*,"[34] the expression *tajjalān* is interpreted by Śaṅkara to mean that (*tat*) which gave rise to (*ja*) the world, reabsorbs (*li*) it and supports (*an*) it. The *Taittirīya* explicitly says that *Brahman* is the cause of the origination, sustentation and destruction of the universe. The *Īśa* and the *Kena Upaniṣads* together seek to establish the causality of *Brahman* in relation to the world. The *Īśa* opens with the statement that all this, meaning the universe, is enveloped by God. That is, the universe derives its substance from God. The *Kena* teaches that *Brahman* is the prime mover of all things. The very first word *kena* (*by whom?*), from which the *Upaniṣad* gets its name, is cast in the instrumental case, showing thereby that the Scripture is concerned with the teaching about the efficient cause of the universe.

From the relevant texts it is clear that *Brahman* is the whole cause of the universe. That out of which the universe is made is the same as that which makes it. For the world, *Brahman* is both the material cause and the efficient cause. Let us illustrate. In the *Taittirīya* it is said: "He desired, 'May I procreate myself.' He performed austerity. Having performed austerity, he created all this, whatever there is here. Having created, into it, indeed, he entered."[35] The *Chāndogya*, similarly, declares, "It thought: 'Would that I were many! Let me procreate myself!' ", and then proceeds to describe the emergence of fire, water and food in succession.[36] The *Bṛhadāraṇyaka* describes how the world was at first unmanifest, and how later it was made manifest through names (*nāma*) and forms (*rūpa*). Having manifested the world, the self, in the words of the *Upaniṣad*, entered it, even to the nail-tips, as a razor would be hidden in a razor-case, or fire in a fire-holder.[37] The manifestation of the world out of *Brahman* is likened to the ejection of the thread from a spider, or the scattering of sparks from fire, to the sprouting of herbs from the earth, and the growth of the hairs of the head and body on a living person. Though the world of plurality has emerged out of the one inner self (*antarātman*), the latter is not affected by the defects of the former. After mentioning the analogies of the one fire and the one wind assuming different forms, the *Kaṭha* says, "As the sun, the eye of all the world, is not sullied by the external defects of the eyes, so the one inner self of all things is not sullied by the misery of the world, being external to it."[38]

From the acosmic standpoint, there is no real creation ; the world is an appearance, it is not real. Such a view naturally involves the notion of *māyā*, the principle which accounts for the apparent conditioning of the unconditioned Absolute. It is true that the doctrine of *māyā* is not to be found in the *Upaniṣads* in its full-fledged form. But the thought itself is not unknown to some of the seers of the *Upaniṣads.* The teachings of Yājñavalkya, for instance, imply such a notion. The sage declares that where there is duality *as it were* (*iva*), there one sees another, one smells another, one hears another, and so forth ; but where there is no duality, there is no scope for all such empirical usage.[39] Here the expression "as it were" implies that the world of duality is not real, that is illusory, *māyā.* The *Chāndogya* characterizes all modifications to be mere names, verbal expressions (*vācārambhaṇam, nāma-dheyam*).[40] In the *Maitrāyaṇīya,* the Absolute is compared to a wheel of fire, an analogy which was developed later by Gauḍapāda to explain the illusory nature of the world. The term "*māyā*" itself can be traced to the *Ṛg-veda* where the assumption of many shapes by Indra through his illusions (*māyās*) is mentioned.[41] And, it is significant that this text is quoted in the *Bṛhadāraṇyaka* in a context where real difference is denied.[42] When we come to the *Śvetāśvatara,* we find the term *māyā* used in the sense of illusion, and the Lord of all beings is described as *māyin.*[43] As for the term *avidyā* which is an equivalent of *māyā,* it occurs in quite a few of the *Upaniṣad* texts. That the manifestation of the world is a marvel is what terms like *māyā* and *avidyā* tell us.

The production of the pluralistic universe does in no way affect the integrity and absoluteness of *Brahman.* "That is full; this is full. The full comes out of the full. Taking the full, from the full, the full itself remains."

6. THE SOUL AND ITS DESTINY

The individual soul is called *jīva.* The word is derived from the root *jīv,* "to live". According to both the cosmic and the acosmic views, the soul is non-different, in essence, from *Brahman.* It is the psycho-physical outfit with which it is associated during the transmigratory process that makes it appear different as it were; when shorn of this limitation, it will be realized that the soul is the same as the non-dual Spirit.

In the *Taittirīya-upaniṣad,* there is an analysis of the five sheaths in which the soul is enveloped, as it were. The envelopes are *annarasamāyā* which is the outermost sheath made of food, i.e. the physical body ; *prāṇa-māyā,* the sheath of vital air ; *manomāyā* the sheath of mind ; *Vijñāna-māyā,* the sheath of intellect ; and *ānnadamāyā,* the sheath of bliss. In later Vedānta, the first is also known as the gross body (*sthūla-śarīra*), the next three constitute the subtle body (*sūkṣmaśarīra*), and the last is called the causal body (*kāraṇaśarīra*). i.e. ignorance or nescience (*avidyā*). These together constitute "the empirical home" of the soul. Being conditioned by these, the soul becomes the subject of experience and enjoyment. The *Kaṭhopaniṣad* compares the self to the lord of the chariot, the body to the chariot, the intellect to the charioteer, the mind to the reins, the senses to the horses, and the sense-objects to the roads ; and it adds that the individual soul as associated with the body, the senses, and the mind, is the experient or enjoyer (*bhoktā*).[44]

In all experience the mind or *manas*, of course, is the central factor. The *Bṛhadāraṇyaka* enumerates the main functions of the mind—desire, resolve, doubt, faith, lack of faith, steadfastness, lack of steadfastness, shame, intellection, fear—and says that all these are *manas* only.[45] The mind functions through the sense-organs which are ten in number—five of cognition, viz., the organs of sight *(cakṣus)*, hearing *(śrotra)*, touch *(tvak)*, taste *(rasana)* and smell *(ghrāṇa)*; and five of action, viz., the organs of speech *(vāk)*, grasping *(pāṇi)*, moving (*pāda*) excretion (*pāyu*) and generation (*upastha*), *Manas,* as the central organ of consciousness, gathers knowledge through the cognitive sense-organs, integrates the pieces of information thus gathered, and acts with the aid of one or more of the organs of action.

The soul, in the view of the *Upaniṣads,* is not born with the body, nor does it perish therewith. "The wise one (i.e. the soul) is not born; nor does it die. This one has not come from anywhere ; nor has it become anyone. Unborn, constant, eternal, primeval, this one is not slain when the body is slain."[46] What happens at death is only the decease of the physical body. The soul migrates from life to life, being conditioned by the cause of such migration, i.e. ignorance, and by the instrument which enables it to migrate, i.e. the subtle body. We first meet with a clear reference to the transmigration-doctrine in the *Bṛhadāraṇyaka*. Asked as to what happens to a dead man after the different components of his body are resolved into the elements like fire, etc., Yājñavalkya is reported to have taken the questioner aside and discoursed on transmigration to him in private. Giving the gist of the discourse, the *Upaniṣad* says, 'What they said was *karma*. What they praised was *karma*. Verily, one becomes good by good works, and evil by evil."[47] In a later context, the same sage explains more fully his view of transmigration. On death, the soul shuffles off its present body and enters a new one, as a caterpillar, having come to the end of a blade of grass, draws itself together and takes a leap to another blade. The process is also comparable to a goldsmith making a newer and more beautiful form like that of the fathers, or of the celestial nymphs, or of the gods, or of Prajāpati, or of Brahmā, or of other beings. The kind of form that the soul takes would depend on its previous *karma*. "As is a man's desire, such is his resolve; as is his resolve, such is the action he performs; what action he performs, that he procures for himself."[48] The transmigration of human soul into the sub-human species is also held to be possible. The *Kaṭhopaniṣad*, for instance, says : 'Some go into a womb for the embodiment of a corporeal being. Others go into what is stationary, according to their deeds, according to their knowledge."[49] The view is also held that when a person dies, he may go to other regions before he takes another birth in this world. Referring to those who are attached to sacrificial forms, the *Muṇḍaka* says, "Having had enjoyment on top of the heaven won by good works, they re-enter this world, or even a lower region."[50]

Anticipations of the *karma*-doctrine are to be found in the Vedic concept of *ṛta* which meant not only the ordered course of things but the moral order as well. The principle of *karma* is the counterpart in the moral realm of the physical law of causality. But what is worthy of note here is that the philosophy of the *Upaniṣads* postulates the possibility of the soul's release from the cycle of *karma*.

Mokṣa or release is the goal of every soul; and release consists in the soul's freedom from the need to be re-born. There are two views in the *Upaniṣads* regarding the nature of the goal. According to one of them, *mokṣa* is attainable only after death; and according to the other, it can be attained here in this very life. The former of these views is, in effect, an inheritance from the eschatological doctrines of the *Mantras* and the *Brāhmaṇas,* according to which heaven is a far-off place which could be reached by the soul only after it has cast off its physical body. But this view undergoes a great transformation as it appears in the *Upaniṣads.* The ideal is no longer a becoming something which one is not, but, attaining *Brahman* with which the soul is identical in essence. "Into *Brahman* which is the soul of mine," says the seer of *Upaniṣad*, "I shall enter on departing hence."[51] The soul which thus realizes its identity with *Brahman* is said to go by the path of the gods (*devayāna*), which is different from the path of the fathers *(piṛtyāna)* which is for the bound soul still in the course of transmigration The other view of the goal, which is in accord with the acosmic conception of the Absolute, is that release is not a state to be newly attained, as it is the eternal nature of the self. When ignorance which is the cause of bondage is dispelled by wisdom, the soul realizes its non-difference from *Brahman* ; and this is release which, therefore, need not wait till the decease of the body. "When all the desires that abide in one's heart are cast away, then a mortal becomes immortal ; he attains *Brahman here.*"[52] "His *prāṣṇas* do not depart. Being *Brahman*, he attains *Brahman.*"[53] So far as the content of release is concerned, it is to be noted, there is no difference between the two views. *Mokṣa* is release from bondage, freedom from *saṁsāra*. It is not a mere negative state of absence of sorrow ; it is absolute bliss, undisturbed peace.

The course of life that a man should adopt in order to be able to attain *mokṣa* is outlined in several of the *Upaniṣad* texts. Generally, the *Upaniṣads* assume on the part of the aspirant a high grade of ethical culture. Because the moral life is assumed as a condition precedent for inquiry into *Brahman–Ātman*, the *Upaniṣads* do not elaborate on ethical codes. But even as it is, there are many texts where, in unmistakable terms, good life is insisted upon. In view of this, it is ununderstandable how it could be maintained, as does Keith, that "in comparison with the intellectual activity of the Brahmans the ethical content of the *Upaniṣads* must be said to be negligible and valueless",[54] and that "the aims of the Brahmans were bent on things which are not ethical at all". In *Upaniṣads* like the *Taittirīya*, instructions are to be found even as regards the most ordinary rules that an individual should adopt in his dealings with others. In the *Bṛahdāraṇyaka*, an entire philosophy of ethics is given in the form of the *da-da-da* sound of thunder. The three *da's* stand for the three imperatives: *dāmyata, datta,* and *dayadhvam,* meaning "Cultivate self-control", "Be generous," and "Have compassion." The three classes of beings, gods, men, and demons, according to the Upaniṣadic episode, understood the sound *da* to signify one of the three commands in the order mentioned. But this does not mean, as Śaṅkara takes care to point out, that the humans have to practise generosity alone and not the other virtues. All the three commands are meant for them; for there are no gods or demons other than men. It will be of some interest to note that T. S. Eliot makes "What the Thunder said" the theme of the last section of his poem *The Wasteland* whose last few lines read as follows :

> "These fragments I have shored against my ruins.
> Why then Ile fit you. Hieronymo's mad againe.
> Datta, Dayadhvam, Dāmyata
> Shantih Shantih Shantih.'

Forgetfulness of the true nature of the self is, according to *Upaniṣads*, the foundation of bondage. This brings about the soul's wrong identification with the ego, mind and body; and in consequence thereof, the soul is caught in the wheel of birth and death. The path to release must naturally be a reverse process. The soul has first to withdraw itself from the narrow limitations of empirical existence, by breaking the walls of finitude. This has to be accomplished by the cultivation of the spirit of renunciation *(vairāgya* or *tyāga)*. But renunciation could be complete only with the dawn of knowledge. It is through knowledge of *Brahman* that ignorance is finally overcome. The knowledge that is referred to here is not to be identified with discursive thought or theoretical appreciation of the non-quality of the self. *Brahman* is to be known by *being* it. The process of realizing *Brahman* is through three stages. *śravaṇa*, *manana* and *nididhyāsna*. The first stands for the study of the *Upaniṣads* under a proper guide. The second requires an intellectual conviction in what the *Upaniṣads* teach obtained through untiring reflection and logical analysis. The third stage which is continued meditation leads to the final wisdom. As aids to contemplation, many modes of meditation known as *vidyā* are taught in the *Upaniṣads*. The aim of all such discipline is to lead the aspirant to the knowledge of the non-dual reality. "If a person knew the self as 'I am He', then, with what desire, for love of what would he cling to the body ?"[55]

NOTES

1. The title of J. Mascaro's translations from the Sanskrit of the Principal Upaniṣads (John Murray, London, 1938).
2. *Harijan*. March 2, 1940, p. 23.
3. See Maurice Bloomfield *The Religion of the Veda* (1908), p.55.
4. Paul Deussen, *The Elements of Metaphysics*, tr. by C. M. Duff (Macmillan & Co. Ltd., London, 1894), p. 337.
5. See *The Upanishads*, with English translation by T. M. P. Mahadevan (G. A. Natesan & Co., Madras), p. xxx.
6. *Bṛhadāraṇyaka*, IV, iv, 19.
7. *Pragmatism*, p. 153.
8. See S. S. Suryanarayana Sastri, *Sankaracharaya* (G.A. Natesan & Co., Madras), p. iv.
9. *Chāndogya*, VI, i, 4.
10. *Kaṭha*, ii, 4.
11. *Śvetāśvatara*, V, 1.
12. *Bṛhadāraṇyaka*, II, iv, 12–14.
13. *Ibid.*, III, iv, 2.
14. *Kena*, i, 3.
15. *Taittirīya*, ii, 4.
16. *Bṛhadāraṇyaka*, IV, iv, 20.
17. *Kaṭha*, vi, 13.
18. *Ibid.*, ii, 7.
19. Paul Deussen, *The Philosophy of the Upanishads* (T. & T. Clark, Edinburgh, 1919), p. 39.

20. *Chāndogya*, V, xi, 1.
21. *Bṛhadāraṇyaka*, III, vii, 15.
22. *Taittirīya*, III, i, 1.
23. *Chāndogya*, VIII, i, 5.
24. *Chāndogya*, VI, viii, 7.
25. *Ibid*, III, xiv, 2–3.
26. *Ibid*., VII, xxv, 2.
27. *Aitāreya*, V, 3.
28. *Bṛhadāraṇyaka*, III, vii, 8.
29. *Kauṣītakī*, iii 15.
30. *Bṛhadāraṇyaka*, II, i, 20.
31. *Kauṣītakī*, iii, 15.
32. *Bṛhadāraṇyaka*,III, ix, 28.
33. *Taittirīya*, ii, 1.
34. *Chāndogya*,III, xiv, 1.
35. *Taittirīya*, ii, 6.
36. *Chāndogya*, VI, ii, 3–4.
37. *Bṛhadāraṇyaka*, I, iv, 7.
38, *Kaṭha*, V, 9–11.
39. *Bṛhadāraṇyaka*, II, iv, 14.
40. *Chāndogya*, VI, i, 3f.
41. *Ṛg-veda*, VI, 47,48.
42. *Bṛhadāraṇyaka*, II, v, 19.
43. *Bṛahdāraṇyaka*, I, v, 3.
44. *Kaṭha*, iii, 3–4.
45. *Bṛahdāraṇyaka*, I, v, 3.
46. *Kaṭha*, ii, 18.
47. *Bṛhadāraṇyaka*, III, ii, 13.
48. *Ibid*., IV, iv, 3–5.
49. *Kaṭha*, v, 7.

50. *Muṇḍaka*, I, ii, 10.
51. *Chāndogya*, III, xiv, 4.
52. *Kaṭha*, vi, 14.
53. *Bṛhadāraṇyaka*, IV, iv, 6.
54. A. B. Keith, *The Religion and Philosophy of the Veda and Upaniṣads* (Harvard Oriental Series, 1925), p, 584.
55. *Bṛahdāraṇyaka*, IV, iv, 12.

1

ĪŚĀVĀSYA-UPANIṢAD

[*The Īśāvāsya-upaniṣad, or the Īśa-upaniṣad as it is briefly called, which belongs to the Vājasaneyī School of the Yajur-veda, consists of eighteen stanzas. It deals with the problem of the material causality of the world and of man's relation thereto, the nature of the highest truth and the difference between reality and unreality and between knowledge and ignorance. The Upaniṣad derives its name from the opening word of the text, Īśāvāsyam or Īśa. This is one of the most beautiful Upaniṣads and has appealed to thinkers more strongly than any other Upaniṣad. It is beautiful both in thought and in expression.*]

PEACE CHANT

That is full; this is full. The full comes out of the full. Taking the full from the full, the full itself remains. Om peace, peace, peace.

1

By the Lord is encompassed all this, whatsoever changing there is in this changing (world). Through the renunciation of that (world) mayest thou enjoy; covetest thou not anyone's riches.

2

Ever performing works here one may wish to live a hundred years. In this way—not otherwise than this it is—to thee, that art a man, the deed adheres not.

3

There are verily these demoniac worlds, enveloped in blinding darkness; and to them go, departing hence, whosoever slay the self.

4

Unmoving, one, swifter than the mind; the gods do not reach it (the self) as it speeds before; it overtakes others that run, though itself standing still; in it the all-pervading air supports the activities of beings.

5

It moves and it moves not; it is far and it is near; it is inside of all this; and it is outside of all this.

6

And he, who uniformly sees all beings even in his self and his own self in all beings, does not feel repelled therefrom (*i.e.*, from beings).

7

Where to one who knows, all beings are verily

identical with one's own self, there what delusion and what sorrow can be to him who has seen the identity ?

8

He has pervaded all, he who is bright, incorporeal, scatheless, veinless, pure and unsmitten by sin. The seer, wise, pervader, born of himself, he has distributed duly the objects through eternal years.

9

Into blinding darkness enter those who attach themselves to nescience. And they that delight in knowledge appear as entering still greater darkness.

10

Distinct, they say, is what is meant by knowledge and distinct, they say, is what is meant by nescience. Thus have we heard from those wise persons who have discriminated that for us.

11

Knowledge and nescience, he who knows them both together crosses death through knowledge.

12

Into blinding darkness enter those who attach themselves to the unreal. And they that delight in the real appear as entering still greater darkness.

13

Distinct, they say, is what results from the

real and distinct, they say, is what results from the unreal. Thus have we heard from the wise who have discriminated them for us.

14

The real and the unreal, he who knows them both together crosses death through the unreal and attains immortality through the real.

15

With a golden bowl remains closed the face of Truth. Uncover it, O Pūṣan, so that I, devoted to truth, may behold (it).

16

O Pūṣan, one seer without a second, Yama, Sūrya, progeny of Prajāpati, spread out and bring together the rays. May I behold that light which is thy loveliest form ! He who is that Puruṣa, he I am.

17

(May) the wind (enter into) the immortal breath; then (may) this body be reduced to ashes ! Om, intellect, remember what has been done; remember, O intellect; remember what has been done; remember !

18

O Agni, lead us on to prosperity along the auspicious path, knowing, god, all our deeds ! Keep away from us deceitful sin ! We shall offer unto thee words of obeisance again and again.

2

KENA-UPANIṢAD

[*The Kena-upaniṣad belonging to the Sāma-veda is a small text in four sections dealing essentially with the nature of Brahman as the efficient cause, and the knowledge thereof. The central point is that Brahman is not what can come within the scope of our ordinary knowledge. The Upaniṣad derives its name from the first word in the text, namely, kena (by whom.)*]

PEACE CHANT

May my limbs grow vigorous, my speech, breath, eye, ear, also my strength and all my senses ! All is the Brahman of the Upaniṣads. May I never discard Brahman ! May not Brahman discard me ! May there be no discarding of me ! Therefore, let those dharmas which are in the Upaniṣads be in me dedicated to Ātman; let them be in me. Om peace, peace, peace.

(i, 1)

By whom urged does the mind, well urged, alight (on its objects)? By whom directed does the first breath go forth? By whom urged do men utter the speech? The eye and the ear, which god indeed directs?

(i, 2)

It is that which is the ear of the ear, the mind of the mind, the speech, indeed, of the speech, the breath of the breath, the eye of the eye. Having abandoned (the sense of self in these) and departing from this world, the wise become immortal.

(i, 3)

Thither the eye does not go, speech does not go, nor the mind. We do not know, we do not understand, how one can teach this.

(i, 4)

Other than the known, verily, it is, and also above the unknown. Thus have we heard from the ancients who have explained it to us.

(i, 5)

What cannot be expressed through speech, and whereby speech is expressed, that alone, know ye, as Brahman; not this which people worship here.

(i, 6)

What one cannot contemplate with the mind, and whereby, they say, the mind is contemplated, that alone, know ye, as Brahman; not this which people worship here.

Here follow three further stanzas, identical in wording with the above two stanzas and dealing with the eye, the ear and the breath.

(ii, 1)

If thou thinkest, "I know well," only little in truth thou knowest of Brahman's form, which (form) of that (Brahman) exists among gods. Hence it is indeed to be inquired into by thee.

(The disciple): I think it has been known.

(ii, 2)

I do not think I know it well; nor do I know that I do not know it. He, who among us knows it, knows it, and he knows not too that he does not know.

(ii, 3)

He by whom it is not contemplated, by him it is contemplated. He by whom it is contemplated, knows it not. It is not understood by those who understand it. It is understood by those who do not understand it.

(ii, 4)

When it is contemplated as known in every cognition, one attains, indeed, immortality. By the self one attains vitality. By knowledge one attains the immortal.

(ii, 5)

If here a man knows it, then truth there is; and if here he knows it not, there is great destruction. Discerning (it) in beings after beings, the wise become immortal on departing from this world.

(iii, 1)

Once Brahman won a victory for the gods. By that victory of Brahman, the gods attained glory. They felt : "Ours alone is victory, ours alone this glory."

(ii, 2-3)

Brahman, indeed, knew this (false pride) of theirs. He appeared before them. They did not know what spirit (*yakṣa*) it was. They spoke to Agni : "O knower of beings (*jātavedas*), find this out, what this spirit is."

(iii, 4)

Saying that (he would do) so, he ran after that. He (the spirit) asked him (Agni) : "Who art thou?" He replied : "I am verily Agni. I am the knower of beings (*jātavedas*)."

(iii, 5)

(He again asked) : "What vitality (is there) in thee?" (He replied) : "Even all this I can burn, what (there is) on earth."

(iii, 6)

He placed a (blade of) grass before him, (and said) : "Burn this." He approached it with all his speed. He was not able to burn it. He even returned thence. (He told the gods): "I was not able to know what this spirit is."

Then the gods sent Vāyu to find out the identity of the spirit. Vāyu was not able to lift up the grass, though he said that he could lift anything on earth. Vāyu also returned, having failed in his mission. Then they sent Indra for the purpose; but the spirit vanished before him.

(iii, 12)

Then in the same etherial region, he (Indra) came across a woman who was shining intensely, Umā the daughter of Himavān. He asked her: "What spirit is this?"

(iv, 1)

She replied: "(It is) Brahman." (And she added): "Through the victory of Brahman, verily, you (gods) have attained glory." Then, indeed, he knew that (it was) Brahman.

(iv, 2)

Therefore these gods, namely, Agni, Vāyu and Indra, far surpass, as it were, the other gods. They have, indeed, come into very intimate contact with him (Brahman). They, indeed, for the first time knew that (it was) Brahman.

(iv, 3)

Therefore, Indra, far surpasses, as it were, the other gods. He has, indeed, come into very intimate contact with him (Brahman). He, indeed, for the first time knew that (it was) Brahman.

(iv, 4)

Of this (Brahman) there is this teaching : this is, as it were, the flash of lightning and it has vanished. Thus (the teaching) concerning the gods.

(iv, 5)

Now (the teaching) concerning the self : It is this towards which the mind appears as moving. In association with that, this (self) repeatedly remembers as resolve.

(iv, 6)

That, indeed, is what is called *tadvana* (that desire). As *tadvana* it is to be worshipped. He who knows this (Brahman) thus, him all beings love.

(iv, 7)

"Sir, teach (me) the Upaniṣad."

"(To thee) has been explained the Upaniṣad. Now we will explain to thee the Upaniṣad relating to Brahman."

(iv, 8-9)

Penance, restraint, sacrificial rites, these are its (Upaniṣad) support. The Vedas are all its limbs. Truth is its abode. He who knows it (Upaniṣad) thus, shaking off sin, in the end he is firmly established in the supreme world of heaven; yea, he is firmly established.

3

KAṬHA-UPANIṢAD

[The Kaṭha-upaniṣad is a fairly long text in six parts called Vallīs, divided into two chapters, each chapter consisting of three Vallīs. Here, Death discourses to a young boy called Naciketas upon the problem of "after death." The picture of this young boy facing Death and compelling him to reveal the secret adds a human touch to what may otherwise be a dry philosophical discourse, and the situation then is full of pathos. Those who are familiar with the Bhagavad-gītā will note that many passages in the Gītā are reminiscent of the text of this Upaniṣad. The Upaniṣad belongs to the Thaittirīya School of the Yajur-veda.]

PEACE CHANT

Let it guard both of us; let it protect both of us; let us both work together; let our study be well illumined; let us not dislike each other. Om peace, peace, peace.

(I, i, 1)

Desiring (heavenly rewards), Vājaśravasa, they say, gave away all his possessions. He had a son named Naciketas.

(I, i, 2)

When the gifts (consisting of cows) were being led (to the priests), faith entered him, who was still a boy; he thought :

(I, i, 3)

These cows drink water, eat grass, (once) yielded milk and are (now) barren. Joyless, verily, are those worlds ; to them he (the sacrificer) goes by giving them away.

(I, i, 4)

He said to his father : "O Sire, to whom wilt thou give me away ?" Twice, thrice (he repeated.) Then to him (the father) replied, "Unto Death shall I give thee."

(I, i, 5)

(Naciketas) : Of many I go as the first; of many I go as the middling. What remains for Death to be accomplished that to-day through me he will accomplish ?

(I, i, 6)

Looking back how it was with men of old, looking forward thus with those who come later, like corn does a mortal ripen; like corn does he spring to life again.

(Naciketas went to the abode of Death and he had to wait there for three nights before Death returned and could show him hospitality due to a guest.)

(I, i, 9)

(Death said): O Brahmin, since thou, a venerable guest, hast stayed in my abode three nights without eating, obeisance to thee, O Brahmin; may prosperity be to me. Choose three boons (for the three nights of waiting).

The first two boons chosen by Naciketas are not of any philosophical importance. The first was that his father's anger might be appeased. The second was that he might know the nature of the Agni (Fire) which led those who performed sacrifices to heaven. Both these boons were readily granted by Death. And the boy was asked to choose the third boon.

(I, i, 20)

(Naciketas):

There is this doubt in respect of a man who is dead—some saying, "he is", and others, "he is not". May I know this, instructed by thee? This boon is the third of the boons.

(I, i, 21)

(Death):

The gods of yore had doubts even on this point. It is not, indeed, easy to understand:

(so) subtle is this truth (*Dharma*). Choose another boon, O Naciketas. Do not stand in my way. Release me from this.

(I, i, 22)

(Naciketas) :

The gods, it may be, had doubts even on this point. And thou, O Death, hast declared it to be not easy to understand. And another teacher of this, like thee, is not to be found. There is no other boon equal to this.

(I, i, 23)

(Death) :

Choose sons and grandsons who would live a hundred years, many cattle, elephants, gold, and horses. Choose the great sovereignty over the earth. And thou thyself live as many years as thou wilt.

(I, i, 24)

If thou considerst this as an equal boon, choose wealth and long life. O Naciketas, prosper thou on this vast earth. I will make thee the enjoyer of thy desires.

(I, i, 25)

Whatever desires there are that are difficult to attain in this world of mortals, all those desires thou mayst ask at thy will. Here are lovely maidens, with chariots, with lutes. The like of them are not to be attained by men.

With them bestowed by me, have thee well served. O Naciketas, do not ask about death.

(I, i, 26)

Naciketas :

These may not last till tomorrow. O Death, they wear away the vigour of all the senses of men. All life is small indeed. Thine (be) the vehicles; thine the dance and the music.

(I, i, 27)

Man cannot be propitiated with wealth. We will get wealth if we meet thee : we will live as long as thou shalt rule. But that alone is the boon which I can choose.

(I, i, 28)

Having come to the immortals who never decay, which decaying mortal living on the earth below, (now) knowing, will, thinking of colour, pleasures and enjoyments, delight in the life (that may be) very long ?

(I, i, 29)

In respect of which, O Death, people doubt thus, what there is in that great hereafter, tell us that. This boon which penetrates into the hidden, no other than this will Naciketas choose.

(*Naciketas was firm; and finding him worthy of the teaching, Death begins to explain the great secret to him.*)

(I, ii, 1)

Different is the good, and different, indeed, is the pleasing. These two, having different purposes, bind man. It becomes well with him who accepts the good. But he who chooses the pleasing falls away from the purpose.

(I, ii, 2)

Both the good and the pleasing come to man. One who is wise considers the two all round and discriminates them. He chooses the good in preference to the pleasing. One who is stupid chooses the pleasing for the sake of acquisition and prosperity.

Death explains why people mostly choose the pleasant, and compliments Naciketas on his preferring the good. Then he proceeds with the explanation of the great teaching.

(I, ii, 5)

Remaining in the midst of ignorance, wise in themselves and considering themselve learned, fools go round and round, staggering to and fro, like blind men led by one who too is blind.

(I, ii, 7)

He (the self) who is not available even to be heard of by many, and whom many do not know even when they hear (of him), wonderful is he who teaches him (the self) and skilled is he who attains him; wonderful is he who knows (him) when taught by a skilled (teacher).

After further elaboration of the point, Naciketas asks for instruction on what transcends the duals like dharma and adharma; and Death continues his discourse.

(I, ii, 15)

The word (or goal) which all the Vedas declare, that which all penances proclaim, and desiring which people lead an austere life, that word (or goal) I tell thee in brief : it is *Om.*

(I, ii, 18)

The knowing self is not born; nor does he die. He sprang from nothing and nothing sprang (from him). He is unborn, eternal, everlasting and ancient. He is not slain when the body is slain.

(I, ii, 19)

If the slayer thinks of slaying and if the slain thinks of being slain, both of them do not know. He neither slays nor is he slain.

(I, ii, 20)

Subtler than the subtle, grosser than the gross, the self is concealed in the heart-cave of this creature. He who is free from desire and free from sorrow perceives the glory of the self through the purity of the mind and the senses.

(I, ii, 21)

Sitting he wanders afar; lying he goes everywhere. Who save myself is fit to know that God who rejoices and rejoices not?

(I, ii, 22)

Knowing the self as without body among the embodied, the abiding among the transitory, great and all-pervading, the wise one does not grieve.

(I, ii, 23)

This self cannot be attained through exposition, nor through intellectual power, nor even through vast learning. He whom alone this (self) accepts, by him he is to be attained. To him this self reveals his own nature.

(I, iii, 3)

Know the self as the lord of the chariot and the body as verily the chariot; know the intellect as the charioteer and the mind as verily the reins.

(I, iii, 4)

The senses are the horses, they say; the sense-objects are the spheres for them. (The individual self) as associated with the body, the senses and mind, is the enjoyer : so say the wise men.

(I, iii, 5)

Whoever becomes devoid of knowledge because of mind ever unyoked, for him the senses are uncontrollable, as wild horses are for a charioteer.

(I, iii, 6)

But whoever becomes endowed with knowledge because of mind ever yoked, for him the senses are controllable, as trained horses are for a charioteer.

(I, iii, 7)

Whoever becomes devoid of knowledge without control over the mind and ever impure, does not reach that place, but gets into transmigratory life.

(I, iii, 8)

But whoever becomes endowed with knowledge, with control over the mind and ever pure reaches that place, whence he is not born again.

(I, iii, 10)

Superior to the senses are indeed the objects; and superior to the objects is the mind. Even superior to the mind is the intellect; and superior to the intellect is the Great (*Mahat*), the self.

(I, iii, 11)

Superior to the Great is the Unmanifest; superior to the Unmanifest is the Self. Superior to the Self there is nothing. That is the goal, that the supreme destination.

(I, iii, 14)

Arise, awake; having approached the venerable teachers know (the truth). The sharp edge of a razor is hard to tread. So also that path, the wise declare, is hard to travel.

(I, iii, 15)

Devoid of sound, of touch, of form, without decay, and likewise devoid of taste, eternal and devoid of odour, beginningless, endless, superior to the Great (*Mahat*) and firm; realising that, one is released from the jaws of death.

(I, iii, 16)

This story of Naciketas, narrated by Death, eternal, if an intelligent person narrates it or hears it, he attains glory in the world of Brahmā.

(II, i, 1)

The self-born Lord forced the senses outward; hence one sees outward and not the inner self. Some one who is wise, desiring immortality, saw, the inner self, by turning the eyes inward.

(II, i, 2)

The immature pursue outward pleasures; they are caught in the far-flung snare of death. But the wise, knowing immortality to be permanent, do not pray for anything here amidst what are transitory.

(II, i, 3)

That by which one perceives colour, taste, odour, sounds and conjugal contacts, by that alone does one perceive. What else remains here ?

This verily it is.

(II, i, 4)

That by which one perceives both what is within dreams and what is within the waking state—having known that great, all-pervading self, the wise does not grieve.

(II, i, 6)

He who was born first from penance was born prior to the waters—one sees him well as dwelling along with the elements, having entered the cave of the heart.

This verily it is (that he sees).

(II, i, 8)

Agni, the knower of all (*jātavedas*), concealed between the two firesticks, like the embryo well borne by pregnant women, and deserving of worship day after day by men awake, offering oblations.

This verily it is.

(II, i, 9)

That from which the sun rises and that in which he sets, in that all the gods are placed. No one ever goes beyond that.

This verily it is.

(II, i, 10)

What is here, the same is there. What is there, the same is similarly here. From death to death, he goes who sees here a manifold as it were.

(II, i, 11)

By the mind alone is this to be reached. There is no plurality whatever here. From death to death, he goes who sees here a manifold as it were.

(II, i, 12)

The Person of the size of a thumb rests in the middle of the body. He is the Lord of what has been and what will be. One is not repelled from Him.

This verily it is.

(II, i, 13)

The Person of the size of a thumb is like light without smoke. Lord of what has been and what will be, he alone is today; and he is also tomorrow.

This verily it is.

(II, i, 14)

As rain water falling on a peak runs down the mountains, so he who sees the entities as distinct, simply runs after them.

(II, i, 15)

As pure water poured into pure (water) remains the same, so becomes the self of the seer who understands, O Gautama.

(II, ii, 1)

The city of eleven gates belonging to the unborn of uncrooked intelligence—occupying it, one does not grieve. And being released, he is released, indeed.

This verily it is.

(II, ii, 2)

He is the Swan (sun) dwelling in the bright (heavens), the Vasu (the pervader) dwelling in the interspace; he is the sacrificer dwelling in the altar; he is the guest dwelling in the sacrificial vessel; he dwells in men, in gods, in sacrifices, in the heavens; he is born in water; he is born in cows; he in born in truth; he is born on the mountains; he is the true and the great.

(II, ii, 3)

He raises the *prāṇa* upwards. He throws the *apāna* downwards. The dwarf seated in the middle, all the gods worship.

(II, ii, 4)

Of this soul which resides in the body and which is about to slip away, what remains here when it is released from the body?

This verily it is.

(II, ii, 5)

No man whatsoever lives either by the *prāṇa* or by the *apāna*. By the other they live, on which these two are dependent.

(II, ii, 6)

Well ! I will explain to thee this Brahman that is secret and eternal; and how the self is, O Gautama, after it comes to death.

(II, ii, 7)

Some souls enter a (new) womb to become embodied. Others enter what is stationary (trees, etc.) according to their action, according to their learning.

(II, ii, 8)

This Person who is awake in those that sleep, fashioning desire after desire—that alone is the bright : that is Brahman; that alone is called the immortal. Therein do all the worlds rest. And nothing at all surpasses that.

This verily it is.

(II, ii, 9)

As *Agni* (Fire), which is one, entering this world becomes varied in form according to the respective forms (of the objects it burns), so also the one inner self of all beings becomes varied in form according to the respective forms of beings it inhabits and also (exists) outside.

(II, ii, 11)

As the sun who is the eye of all beings is not stained by the external defects pertaining to the eyes, so also the inner self of all beings is not stained by the misery of beings (though) external.

(II, ii, 12)

The one controller, the inner self of all who makes his one form manifold; the wise who perceived him as existing in themselves—for them there is eternal happiness; not for others.

(II, ii, 13)

The eternal among the eternal, the intelligent among the intelligent beings, the one among the many, who grants desires; the wise who perceive him as existing in themselves—for them there is eternal peace, not for others.

(II, ii, 14)

"That is this"—(thus) they think of the indescribable supreme happiness. How then may I come to know of it, whether it shines (simply), or whether it shines distinctly ?

(II, ii, 15)

Not there does the sun shine, nor the moon and the stars; nor do this lightnings shine. Whence then is this *Agni* (fire) ? Him alone, as he shines, does everything (else) shine after. By this lustre, do all this shine distinctly.

(II, iii, 1)

With roots upward, with branches downward (there stands) this ancient fig-tree. That alone is the bright; that is Brahman; that alone is called the immortal. Therein do all the worlds rest. And nothing at all surpasses that.

This verily it is.

(II, iii, 2)

Whatever world there is moves in *prāṇa*, coming out (of it). It is the great fear, the thunder-bolt held aloft. They who know that become immortal.

(II, iii, 3)

Out of fear for him, *Agni* (fire) burns; the sun burns out of fear (for him). Out of fear (for him), Indra and Vāyu speed on; (and so does) Death as the fifth.

(II, iii, 5)

As in a mirror, so is it seen all round, as it were in the body; as in dream, so in the world of the departed Fathers; as in waters, so in the world of the celestial nymphs ; as in shade and sun, so in the world of Brahman.

(II, iii, 6)

The separate nature of the senses which originate separately, and what forms their rising and sitting—knowing these a wise man does not grieve.

(II, iii, 7)

Superior to the senses is the mind. Superior to the mind is the intellect (buddhi). Superior to the intellect is the Great, the self. Superior to the Great is the unmanifest.

(II, iii, 8)

But superior to the unmanifest is the Person, who is the pervader of all and indeed devoid of marks, and knowing whom the living being gets released and attains immortality.

(II, iii, 10)

When the five-fold (sense) knowledge, along with the mind comes to cessation, and when the intellect too does not wander, that is called the highest attainment.

(II, iii, 11)

This they regard as the Yoga—the steady control of the senses. Then one becomes free from distraction. Yoga indeed is the source and the end.

(II, iii, 12)

Not indeed by speech, nor by mind, nor by the eye is it to be reached. How can it be seen by any other than one who says, "It is"?

(II, iii, 13)

He can be comprehended only as "It is", and also through the real nature of both. The real nature of it manifests itself clearly when it is comprehended only as "It is".

(II, iii, 14)

When all the desires which abide in his heart are cast away, then the mortal becomes immortal. Here he attains Brahman.

(II, iii, 15)

When all the bondages here of the heart break, then the mortal becomes immortal : this much is the Instruction.

(II, iii, 16)

One hundred and one are the channels (*nāḍīs*) of the heart. One among them rises up towards the head. Going up along that, one attains immortality. The others are for getting out in various directions.

(II, iii, 17)

The person of the size of a thumb, the inner self, resides always in the heart of men. Him let a man draw forth from his body with firmness, as one draws the core from a reed. Him let a man know as the bright, the immortal; him let a man know as the bright, the immortal.

(II, iii, 18)

Then, having received this knowledge imparted by Yama, as also the entire procedure of Yoga, Naciketas attained Brahman and became free from blemishes and deathless. So also will it be with any other who knows thus what verily relates to the self.

4

PRAŚNA-UPANIṢAD

[*The Praśna-upaniṣad which belongs to the Atharva Veda contains six sections in the form of six questions put to a ṛṣi by six disciples seeking knowledge of Brahman and the ṛṣi's answers to the questions. Because it consists of questions, the Upaniṣad is called Praśna (Question) Upaniṣad. The ultimate cause of this world, the Supreme Being, the nature and power of the sound Om and the relation of the Supreme to the constituents of the world : these are the subjects dealt with in this Upaniṣad.*]

PEACE CHANT

May we, O gods, hear what is auspicious with our ears ! May we, ye who are deserving of worship, see what is auspicious with our eyes ! With strong limbs and bodies, may we fulfil in worship what life is allotted to us by the gods !

May Indra of waxing glory bestow prosperity on us ! May Pūṣan, knower of all, bestow prosperity on us ! May Tārkṣya of unobstructed path bestow prosperity on us ! May Bṛhaspati bestow prosperity on us !

(i, 1)

Sukēśā son of Bhāradvāja, Satyakāma son of Śibi, Gārgya grandson of Sūrya, Kausalya son of Aśvala, Bhārgava of the Vidarbha country, Kabandhi son of Kātya—these, as mentioned above, devoted to Brahman and intent on Brahman, were in search of the supreme Brahman; and they approached the venerable Pippalāda with sacrificial fuel in their hands, believing that he would tell them all that.

(i, 2)

The ṛṣi said to them :—Live (here) another year with penance, austerity and devotion. (Then) ask questions according to your desire. If we know, then we shall tell you all that.

(i, 3)

After that (a year) Kabandhī son of Kātya approached him and asked :—Venerable sir, whence are all these creatures born ?

(i, 4)

To him he said :—Prajāpati desired to have offspring; he performed penance. Performing penance, he produced the pair, namely, wealth and life, in the hope that these two would procure him variety of offspring.

(i, 5)

The sun indeed is life; wealth itself is the moon. Wealth is verily all this, what is tangible and what is intangible. Therefore the tangible itself is wealth.

(i, 6)

Now, the sun after rising, enters the eastern quarter. Thus he takes in into his rays the vital breaths of the east. Because he illumines all the quarters of south, west, north, below, above and in-between, he takes in into his rays all the vital breaths.

(i, 7-8)

So he rises as Vaiśvānara fire, of cosmic form, the life. This is said in the verse :—Of cosmic form, full of rays, knower of all, the goal (of all), the one effulgence, the giver of heat, possessing a thousand rays, existing in a hundred forms—thus rises this sun as the life of beings.

(i, 9)

Verily, Prajāpati is the year. It has two paths, the southern and the northern. Now those who dedicate themselves to deeds like sacrifices and public benefactions win only the world of the moon. They certainly return again. Therefore the ṛṣis desiring offspring resort to the southern path. This, which is called the path of the dead ancestors, is the wealth.

(i, 10)

But those who search for the self along the northern path with penance, austerity, devotion and knowledge, win the sun. This is the abode of the vital breaths This is immortal ; (this is) free from fear. This is the goal. From this they do not return again. Thus is this denied (to the ignorant).

(i, 11)

Here there is this verse :—They speak of him as the father having five feet, and twelve forms, as the source of water, (existing) in the higher half of the heavens. And others again speak of him as the omniscient placed on (a chariot of) seven wheels and six spokes.

(i, 12)

Prajāpati verily is the month. Of this, the dark half is the wealth, the bright half is life. Hence the ṛṣis perform sacrifices in the other (half).

Here there is a similar statement about day and night, and about food, identifying day with life and night with wealth, and identifying food with Prajāpati.

(i, 15)

Thus those (householders) who observe the vow of Prajāpati produce the couple (son and daughter). For them alone is this world of Brahmā, who perform penance and observe austerity, and in whom truth is well established.

(i, 16)

This world of Brahmā free from blemishes is for them in whom there is no crookedness and untruth, nor deceit.

(ii, 1)

Then Bhārgava of the Vidarbha country asked him :—Venerable sir, how many gods verily support the created ? How many illumine this ? And who again among them is the supreme ?

(ii, 2)

To him he said :—That god indeed, is ether, air, fire, water, earth, speech, mind, eye and ear. Illuminating (the world) they say; "We alone hold together and support this arrow (the created world)."

(ii, 3)

Life, the greatest of them, said to them : "Do not entertain this false notion. I alone, dividing myself five-fold, hold together and support this arrow."

(ii, 4-5)

They remained indifferent to it. Through indignation, he appeared as departing upward. When he departed, then the others also departed. And when he settled down, others also settled down.

Thus, as when the king of the honey-bees departs (from the hive), all the bees also depart, and when he settles down all of them also settle down, similarly do speech and mind, the eye and the ear.

They were satisfied and praised life thus :— He burns as fire; he is the sun, he is the bountiful rain-god; he is Vāyu. He is the earth, wealth, god. He is also the real and the unreal and what is immortal.

(ii, 6)

As spokes in the nave of a wheel, everything is established in life; the Ṛks, Yajus, and Sāmans, sacrifice, valour and wisdom.

(ii, 7)

You move into the womb as Prajāpati. You yourself are born again. O life, the creatures bring tribute to you who remain well established along with the vital breaths.

(ii, 8)

You are the best bearer (of gifts) to the gods and the first offering to the departed forefathers. You are the life (dedicated to) truth of the ṛṣis, the Atharvāṅgirasas.

(ii, 9)

You are, O life, Indra by your valour; you are Rudra the protector. You move in the interspace; you are the sun, the lord of the luminaries.

(ii, 10)

When you pour down rain, then these creatures breathe; they live in a state of bliss, hoping that there would be food according to their desire.

(ii, 11)

You are ever pure, O life, the one seer (a form of fire), the eater, the good lord of all. We are the givers of what is to be eaten. O all-prevading air, you are our father.

(ii, 12)

That body of yours which is well established in the speech, in the ear and in the eye, which exists continuously in the mind, make that auspicious; do not depart.

(ii, 13)

All this is under the control of life, which is well established in the three worlds. Protect us as a mother does her sons. Give us prosperity and wisdom.

(iii, 1)

Then Kausalya son of Aśvala, also asked him :—O revered sir, whence is this life born ? How does it come into this body ? And after dividing itself, how does it establish itself ? In what way does it depart ? How does it support what is without ? How (does it support) what relates to the self ?

(iii, 2)

To him he said :—You are asking questions (highly) transcendental. Because you are well established in Brahman, I will tell you.

(iii, 3)

This life is born from the self. Just as there is this shadow in (the case of) a person so is this (life) connected therewith. It comes into this body by the activity of the mind.

(iii, 4)

Just as the emperor himself allots to his officers "You occupy these villages (and you) these" even similarly this life allocates the other vital breaths to their respective places.

Here there is a description of the vital breaths and their positions and functions.

(iii, 8)

The sun, indeed, is the external life; for he rises gracing the life that is in the eye.

(iii, 11-12)

The wise one who knows life thus, to him there shall be no lack of offspring. He becomes immortal. Here there is the verse :—

The birth, the coming, the abode, the five-fold overlordship and the nature of being the self, knowing these about life, one attains the immortal; knowing these one attains the immortal.

(iv, 1)

Then Gārgya, the grandson of Sūrya, asked him :—Venerable sir, what are they that sleep in this person ? What are they that keep awake in him ? What god is it that sees dreams ? Whose is this happiness ? In whom are all these established ?

(iv, 2)

To him he said :—O Gārgya, as all the rays of the setting sun become one in this disc of light, and as they spread out when he rises again and again, so does all this become one in the supreme god, the mind.

Therefore at that time the person hears not, sees not, smells not, tastes not, touches not; he speaks not, takes not, rejoices not, evacuates not, moves not. (Then) they say "He sleeps".

Here there is a description of the fire-like vital breaths that ever keep awake.

(iv, 6)

When he becomes overpowered by light, then in this state, that god sees no dreams. Then at that time, that happiness arises in this body.

(iv, 7)

O beloved one, just as birds settle themselves on the trees, their abode, similarly all this is established in the supreme self.

(iv, 9)

He verily, is the seer, the toucher, the hearer, the smeller, the taster, the thinker, the knower, the doer, the person of the nature of intelligence. He establishes himself in the supreme indestructible self.

(iv, 10)

He who knows the shadowless, bodiless, colourless, pure, indestructible (self), attains verily the supreme, indestructible (self). He who (knows thus), O beloved one, becomes omniscient, (becomes) all.

(iv, 11)

Here there is the verse :—

He who knows that indestructible (self) in which are established the self of the nature of intelligence, the vital breaths and the elements along with all the gods, becomes, O beloved one, omniscient and enters all.

(v, 1)

Then Satyakāma, son of Śibi, asked him :—Venerable sir, he who verily, among men meditates till the end of his life on the sound Om—what world indeed does he conquer thereby ?

(v, 2)

To him, he said :—That which is the sound Om, O Satyakāma, is verily the higher and the lower Brahman. Therefore with this support alone does a wise man reach the one or the other.

(v, 3)

If he should meditate on this as of one *mātra*, he, enlighted even by that, soon attains this earthly world. The Ṛks lead him to the world of men. There, becoming rich in penance, austerity and faith, he enjoys supremacy.

(v, 4)

Then, if (he should meditate on this) as of two *mātras*, he attains the mind; he is led to the interspace, the world of the moon, by Yajus. Enjoying supernatural powers there, he returns again.

(v, 5)

But he who should meditate on this supreme self itself with the Om of three *mātras*, becomes one with the light, the sun.

Just as a snake is bereft of its skin, similarly he is freed from sins and is led upward by verses of Sāma to the world of Brahmā. He sees the person, living in the heart and superior to the higher life-mass (Hiraṇyagarbha),

(v, 6)

Here there are two verses :—

The three *mātras*, (each) leading to death (by itself), if they are united to each other without being split up, and used in rites well performed, external, internal or in-between, then the knower does not waver.

(v, 7)

By Ṛks one attains this world. By Yajus (one attains) the interspace. By Sāmans (one attains) what the seers know. That, even by the mere sound Om as support, the wise one attains, and also that which is serene, undecaying, deathless, fearless and supreme.

(vi, 1)

Then Sukeśas, son of Bharadvāja, asked him :—Venerable sir, Hiraṇyanābha, a prince of the Kosala Kingdom, approached me and asked this question : "Do you know, son of Bharadvāja, the person having sixteen parts ?" I replied to that prince: "I know him not. If I had known him, why should I not tell you about it ?" He withers, verily, to his roots who speaks untruth. Hence it behoves me not to speak untruth. In silence, he mounted his chariot and departed. I ask you about him; where is that person ?

(vi, 2)

To him he said :—Even here, within the body, O beloved one, is that person in whom these sixteen parts arise.

(vi, 3)

He (the person) thought :—In whose departure shall I be departing ? And in whom settling down, shall I be settling down ?

(vi, 4)

He created life. From life, faith; (then followed) space, air, light, water, earth, sense-organ, mind, food. From food (sprang) vitality, penance, hymns, work, worlds. And in the worlds (he created) name.

(vi, 5)

As these flowing rivers tending towards the ocean, on reaching the ocean, disappear, their name and form are broken up, and one speaks only of the ocean; even so these sixteen parts of the seer, tending towards the person, on reaching the person, disappear, their name and form are broken up, and one speaks only of the person. That one is what has no parts and what is immortal.

(vi, 6)

Here there is the verse :—

In whom the parts are well established as spokes in the nave of the wheel, know him, the person to be known, so that death may not hurt you.

(vi, 7-8)

To them he (again) said :—Only thus far do I know of this supreme Brahman. There is nothing higher than this. They worshipped him (and said) : Thou, indeed, art our father who dost take us across to the other shore of nescience.

Salutation to the supreme ṛṣis; salutation to the supreme ṛṣis !

5

MUṆḌAKA-UPANIṢAD

[*The Muṇḍaka-upaniṣad belonging to the Atharva-veda, consists of three parts called Muṇḍakas, each sub-divided into two sections. This Upaniṣad draws a clear line between the higher knowledge of the supreme Brahman and the lower knowledge of the phenomenal world. It describes the phenomenal world as springing from the supreme Brahman, regards the benefits of virtues like sacrifices and benefactions as but transitory, and holds up the knowledge of Brahman as thc summum bonum. The Śānti is the same as in the Praśna-upaniṣad.*]

(I, i, 1)

Brahmā arose as the first among the gods—the maker of the universe, the protector of the world. He expounded the knowledge of Brahman, the foundation of all knowledge, to Atharvan, his eldest son.

(I, i, 2)

That knowledge of Brahman—of the higher and the lower—which Brahmā taught to Atharvan, Atharvan (in his turn) expounded to Aṅgir in olden times. He expounded it to Satyavāha, son of Bhāradvāja; the son of Bhāradvāja (expounded it) to Aṅgiras.

(I, i, 3)

Śaunaka, the great householder, duly approached Aṅgiras and asked :—Through what being known, O venerable sir, does all this become known ?

(I, i, 4)

To him he said :—Two kinds of knowledge are to be known—so indeed the knowers of Brahman declare—the higher as well as the lower.

(I, i, 5)

Of these, the lower, (knowledge) is the Ṛg-veda, the Yajur-veda, the Sāma-veda, the Atharva-veda, Phonetics, Ritual, Grammar, Etymology, Metrics and Astronomy. And the higher is that by which the Immutable is known.

(I, i, 7)

As the silk-spider sends forth and withdraws (its thread), as herbs grow on the earth, as the hair (grows) on the head and on the body of a living person, so from the Immutable arises here the universe.

(I, i, 8)

Through penance Brahman expands. Thence food is produced. From food (arises) life; (thence) mind; (thence) the reals (*i.e.*, the five elements); (thence) the worlds; (there the rituals), and in the rituals immortality.

(I, i, 9)

He who knows all and perceives all, whose penance is of the nature of knowledge—from him are born this Brahmā (the Hiraṇyagarbha), name, form and food.

(I, ii, 1)

This is that truth :—

The works which the wise men saw in the hymns are variously disseminated in the triad of the Vedas. Perform them always, ye lovers of truth, this your path to the world of good deeds.

(I, ii, 3)

He whose *Agnihotra* sacrifice is not followed by the new moon and the full moon sacrifices by the *Cāturmāsya* (four-month observance) and the *Agrayaṇa* ceremony, he who does not entertain guests (daily), does not give offerings to the fire, does not perform the *Vaiśvadeva* ceremony, and gives offerings (if at all he gives) contrary to rules—(such conduct of his) destroys all his worlds, even unto the seventh.

Here there is an enumeration of the seven kinds of flames of fire.

(I, ii, 5)

(But) whosover performs his duties at proper times, making his offerings in these shining flames, him these offerings lead (through the rays of the sun) to where the sole Lord of the gods abides.

(I, ii, 6)

The radiant offerings invite him with the words "Come, do come", and carry the sacrificer over the sun-beam, honouring him and accosting with the loving words, "Here is your holy world of Brahmā (*i.e.*, heaven) won through good deeds."

(I, ii, 7)

Unsteady, verily, are these boats of the eighteen sacrificial forms, which are declared to be inferior *karma*. Those misguided men who acclaim this with superior joy fall again into old age and death.

(I, ii, 9)

Dwelling in nescience in manifold ways, the immature men conceitedly imagine : "We have attained our goal." Since those who perform rituals do not understand (the truth) through attachment, they fall, overcome by misery, the fruit of their merits having been exhausted.

(I, ii, 10)

Imagining sacrifices and public benefactions as the highest good, no other good do these misguided men know. Having enjoyed on the floor of heaven won by good deeds, they enter again this world or a still lower one.

(I, ii, 11)

But those who practise penance and faith in the forest, tranquil, and living on alms, depart, free from blemishes, through the door of the sun to where dwells the immortal, imperishable Person.

(I, ii, 12)

Deeply pondering over the worlds that are won by *karma*, let a Brahman arrive at non-attachment. That (Brahman-world) which is not made, cannot be (won) through works. For the sake of this knowledge, let him only approach, with sacrificial fuel in hand, a preceptor who is learned in scriptures and who is firmly established in Brahman.

(I, ii, 13)

Unto him who approaches in due form, whose mind is tranquil and who has attained calmness, the wise one teaches in its very truth that knowledge about Brahman whereby one knows the Imperishable Person, the Truth.

(II, i, 1)

This is that truth :—

As from a blazing fire sparks of like forms come forth by thousands, even so from the immutable many kinds of beings, O beloved one, issue forth; and they return thither too.

(II, i, 2)

Divine and formless is the Person; he is without and within and unborn; he is without breath and without mind; he is pure and higher than the high Immutable.

(II, i, 3)

From him are born life, mind and all the sense-organs, (also) ether, air, light, water and earth which is the support of all.

(II, i, 4)

Fire is his head; the sun and the moon are his eyes; space (ether) is his ear; speech is the revealed scriptures. Air is his life, the universe his heart. From his feet the earth (is born); indeed, he is the self of all beings.

(II, i, 6)

From him are born the Ṛks, the Sāmans and the Yajus, religious vows and sacrifices, all the rituals and the gifts, year, the sacrificer and the worlds where the moon makes (things) pure and where the sun (shines).

(II, i, 7)

And from him the gods are born in manifold ways, also celestials and men, beasts and birds, *prāṇa* and *apāna*, rice and barley, penance, faith, truth, austerity and prescriptions.

Here there is a mention of the various other phenomena of Nature that have come out of the Supreme Being.

(II, i, 10)

The Person himself is all this : work, penance, Brahmā, supreme immortality. He who knows that which is placed in the cave (of the heart)—he cuts asunder the knot of nescience here, O beloved one.

(II, ii, 1-2)

Manifest, well-placed, moving verily in the cave (of the heart) : such is the great goal. Therein is centred (all) this which moves and breathes and winks. Know that as being and non-being, as the supreme object to be desired, as the highest beyond human understanding, as luminous, as subtler than the atoms, as that in which the worlds are established and also the inhabitants of the worlds.

This is that immutable Brahman. He is life; and that is speech and mind. That is this real; that is the immortal. That is what is to be hit (*i.e.*, aimed at in knowing). O beloved one, hit it.

(II, ii, 3)

Taking the Upaniṣadic bow as a great weapon, one should place (on it) the arrow sharpened by meditation. Drawing it with a mind engaged in the contemplation of that (Brahman), O beloved one, hit as target that which is verily immutable.

(II, ii, 4)

The *Praṇava* (the syllable Om) is the bow. One's self indeed is the arrow. Brahman is spoken of as the target of that. It is to be hit without making a mistake. Thus one becomes united with it as the arrow (becomes one with the target).

(II, ii, 5)

He in whom the heavens, the earth and the interspace are woven, and also the mind along with all the vital breaths—him alone know as the one self. Leave off other utterances. This is the bridge to immortality.

(II, ii, 7)

He who knows all and perceives all whose is this greatness on the earth—in the divine city of Brahman, in the ether (of the heart) is that self established.

(II, ii, 9)

The knot of the heart is cut, all doubts are dispelled and his deeds (*i.e.*, the residue thereof) perish, when the higher and lower Brahman has been realised.

(II, ii, 12)

Brahman is verily this immortal. In front is Brahman, behind is Brahman; Brahman is to the right and to the left. It spreads both above and below. Brahman is indeed this universe. It is the greatest.

(III, i, 1)

Two birds, ever united companions, cling to the self-same tree. Of these two, one eats the sweet berry. The other looks on without eating.

(III, i, 2)

On the self-same tree, a person immersed (in the sorrows of the world) is deluded and grieves on account of his want of strength. But he becomes free from sorrow, when he sees the other who is worshipped (by many) and who is the Lord, and also his greatness.

(III, i, 3)

When a wise seer sees the golden coloured Creator, the Lord, the Person, Brahman, the source (of all), then shaking off merit and demerit and free from stain, he attains supreme identity (with the Lord).

(III, i, 4)

He is indeed the life that shines forth through all beings. The wise man who knows this ceases to speak of anything else. He sports in himself; he delights in himself. He continues to do work. Such a one is the greatest of those who know Brahman.

(III, i, 6)

Truth alone conquers, not untruth. By truth is laid out the road (known as) the path of the gods, by which the sages who have their desires (fully) realised, proceed to where is that supreme seat of truth.

(III, i, 10)

Whatever world a man of purified nature thinks of in his mind and whatever desires he desires, all those worlds and all those desires he attains. Therefore he who desires prosperity should worship the knower of the self.

(III, ii, 1)

He knows Brahman, the supreme abode, wherein established the world shines brightly.

The wise men who, free from desires, worship the Person, cross this seed (of rebirths).

(III, ii, 2)

He who entertains desires, thinking of them, is born (again) here and there on account of those desires. But in the case of him who has all his desires fully realised and has accomplished the self, all desires vanish even here (on earth).

(III, ii, 4)

This self is not to be attained by one who is devoid of strength, nor through delusion nor even by penance without an aim. But the wise man who makes the attempt with these means—this self of his enters the Brahman-abode.

(III, ii, 6)

The ascetics who have ascertained well the import of the Vedānta-knowledge and who have purified their natures through the path of renunciation—all of them, the supreme immortals, are liberated at the end of time in the worlds of Brahmā.

(III, ii, 7)

Gone are the fifteen parts to their (respective) supports (*i.e.*, the elements), and all the gods (the sense-organs) into their corresponding deities. One's deeds and the self of the nature of knowledge, all become one in the supreme immutable being.

(III, ii, 9)

He, verily, who knows that supreme Brahman, becomes Brahman itself. In his family there will be born no one who does not know Brahman. Sorrow he crosses; sins he crosses. Liberated from the knots of the cavity (of the heart), he becomes immortal.

(III, ii, 10)

This is said in the verse:—

Those who perform the rites, who are learned in scriptures, who are well established in Brahman, who offer, of themselves, oblations to the one-seer (a form of fire) with faith, to them alone one may expound this knowledge of Brahman, (to them alone) by whom the rite (of carrying fire) on the head has been performed according to rule.

(III, ii, 11)

This aforesaid truth the seer Aṅgiras expounded in former times. One who has not done the rite (of carrying fire on the head) shall not learn this. Salutation to the supreme seers; salutation to the supreme seers.

6

MĀṆḌŪKYA-UPANIṢAD

[*The Māṇḍūkya-upaniṣad belongs to the Atharva-veda. In the form in which it is extant at present, it consists of twelve passages. Here the supreme Brahman is identified with the sound Om, and the whole universe is represented as a manifestation of this Om. The sound Om consists of three elements, namely, A, U and M; and they are identified with Vaiśvānara, Taijasa and Prājña, the presiding sentiences of the three avasthās. There are Kārikās on this Upaniṣad by Gauḍapāda, the earlist known Advaitin, who was the grand-teacher of Śaṅkara; and there is a commentary on the Upaniṣad and the Kārikās by Śankara. The Śānti is the same as in Praśna-upaniṣad.*

(1)

All this is that syllable Om. (Here follows) an explanation of that. What has been, what is and what will be—all this is only the sound Om. And what other there is beyond the threefold time—that too is only the sound Om.

(2)

For, all this is Brahman. This self is Brahman. That self of this nature consists of four parts.

(3)

The first part is Vaiśvānara whose place is in the waking state, who beholds the external objects, who has seven limbs and nineteen mouths and who is the enjoyer of what is gross.

(4)

The second part is Taijasa whose place is in the dream state, who beholds the internal objects, who has seven limbs and nineteen mouths and who experiences the subtle objects.

(5)

That state is deep sleep, where one, being fast asleep, does not desire any desire whatsoever, and does not see any dream whatsoever. The third part is Prājña whose place is in the state of deep sleep, who has become one who is all a mass of sentience, who is of the nature of bliss, who is the enjoyer of bliss and whose mouth is the mind.

(6)

He is the lord of all; he is the omniscient; he is the inner controller; he is the source of all; he is the beginning and end of all beings.

(7)

Not cognising the internal objects, not cognising the external objects, not cognising either, not being a mass of sentience, not cognising and not not-cognising, invisible, incapable of being spoken of, not capable of being grasped, not having any identifying mark, unthinkable, unnamable, the essence of the knowledge of the one self, that into which all phenomena get resolved, tranquil, blissful, non-dual—such they consider as the fourth (part). He is the self. He is to be known.

(8)

That self of this nature is the sound Om, when regarded as word; (and the sound Om rests) in its elements. The parts are the elements and the elements are the parts, namely, the sound *a*, the sound *u* and the sound *m*.

(9)

Vaiśvānara whose place is in the waking state, is the sound *a*, which is the first element, either from the root *āp* (to obtain) or because it has *ādi* (beginning). Indeed he who knows it thus obtains all his desires and he also becomes the first.

(10)

Taijasa whose place is in the dream state, is the sound *u*, which is the second element, because of elevation or because of (equality between) the two. Indeed he who knows it thus elevates the continuity of his knowledge, and he becomes equal; in his family is born no one who does not know Brahman.

(11)

Prājña whose place is in the state of deep sleep is the sound *m*, which is the third element, either from the root *mi* (to measure) or because of merging. Indeed he who knows it thus measures (*i.e.*, knows) all this, and there is merging also (of the entire world in him).

(12)

The fourth is that which has no elements, which cannot be spoken of, into which phenomena get resolved, blissful and non-dual. Thus, the sound Om is the very self. He who knows it thus enters the self with his self.

7

TAITTIRĪYA-UPANIṢAD

[*The Taittirīya-upaniṣad belongs, as is clear from the name, to the Taittirīya school of the Yajur-veda. It is divided into three sections called Vallīs. The first section deals with some mystic problems connected with the text and the study of the Veda. The second deals with the bliss of Brahman and the third deals with the story of Bhṛgu, son of Varuṇa who, under instructions from his father, understands bliss as Brahman through persistent inquiry.*]

PEACE CHANT

May the Sun be auspicious to us and may Varuṇa be auspicious to us. May Aryamān (a form of the Sun) be auspicious to us. May Indra and Bṛhaspati be auspicious to us. May Viṣṇu of wide strides be auspicious to us. Salutation to Brahman. Salutation to Vāyu. Thou, indeed, art the visible Brahman. I shall proclaim thee the real. I shall call thee the truth. Me may that protect; the speaker may that protect. May that protect me; may that proteet the speaker, Om peace, peace, peace.

ŚĪKṢĀ VALLĪ

In this first section, there is little that is of interest from the point of view of the main teaching of the Upaniṣads. There are various mystic statements about the text of the Veda. The following is a specimen :

(I, iii, 1)

Let there be fame for both of us. Let there be the lustre of spiritual knowledge for both of us. Then therefore we propose to explain the mystery of the great *samhitā* in respect of its five supports : in respect of the worlds, in respect of the luminaries, in respect of knowledge, in respect of progeny and in respect of the self. They are spoken of as the great *samhitās*.

Now there is (the explanation) in respect of the worlds : the earth is the fore part; the heaven is the hind part; the inter-space is the middle part; the air is the connection. Thus in respect of the world.

(I, iii, 2)

Now there is (the explanation) in respect of the luminaries : fire is the fore part; the sun is the hind part; water is the middle part; the lightning glow is the connection. Thus in respect of the luminaries.

(I, iii, 3)

Now there is (the explanation) in respect of knowledge : the teacher is the fore part; the disciple is the hind part; knowledge is the middle part; exposition is the connection. Thus in respect of knowledge.

(I, iii, 4)

Now there is (the explanation) in respect of progeny : the mother is the fore part; the father is the hind part; progeny is the middle part; procreation is the connection. Thus in respect of progeny.

(I, iii, 5)

Now there is (the explanation) in respect of the self : the lower jaw is the fore part; the upper jaw is the hind part; speech is the middle part; the tongue is the connection. Thus in respect of the self.

(I, iii, 6)

These are the great *samhitās*. He who understands the great *samhitās* as thus explained, becomes endowed with progeny, with cattle, with the lustre of spiritual knowledge, with food and nourishment and with the heavenly world.

The following are the mantras which the teacher recites, praying for intellectual vigour :

(I, iv, 1)

May that Indra who is the greatest in the Vedas, who is of cosmic form, who has been born of the Vedas, of the immortal (Vedas), enrich me with intellectual vigour. O god, may I become the supporter of the immortal (Vedas).

(May) my body (become) fit. (May) my tongue (be) of supreme sweetness (with knowledge). May I hear much with my two ears. Thou art the sheath of Brahman, covered with intellectual vigour. Protect my learning.

The following are the mantras which the teacher recites for performing homa, praying for prosperity. At the word 'svāhā,' the homa is performed.

(I, iv, 2)

The bringer, the extender, and the long maintainer of her own dresses, cows, food and drink for ever, that prosperity bring me with woolly and other cattle.

May religious students come around unto me, *svāhā*. May religious students come from different parts unto me, *svāhā*. May religious students come unto me duly, *svāhā*. May the religious students be well disciplined, *svāhā*. May the religious students be tranquil, *svāhā*.

(I, iv, 3)

May I be among men of repute, *svāhā*. May I be more renowned among the most wealthy, *svāhā.* O venerable god, may I enter thee, *svāhā.* O venerable god, may thou enter me, *svāhā.* O venerable god, in thee of such thousand branches, I get purified, *svāhā.*

As waters flow downwards, as the months flow into the year, so may religious students come to me, O supporter, from all around, *svāhā.* Thou art a refuge. Shine unto me. Come unto me.

Then comes the final instruction which students in those days received when they completed their study under the teacher. The following is the full text of that instruction, which corresponds to the Convocation addresses of modern times delivered at the Universities to students who are given their degrees at the end of their studies :

(I, xi, 1)

After expounding the Veda, the teacher enjoins the disciple thus : Speak the truth. Practise virtue. Do not neglect the Veda that has been studied. Having brought to the teacher the wealth that is pleasing to him, do not cut off the line of progeny.

Let there be no neglect of truth. Let there be no neglect of virtue. Let there be no neglect of welfare. Let there be no neglect of prosperity. Let there be no neglect of the Veda that has been studied and its teaching. Let there be no neglect of what is due to gods and to departed forefathers.

(I, xi, 2)

Be one to whom mother is a god; be one to whom father is a god; be one to whom teacher is a god; be one to whom guest is a god.

Whatever deeds are blameless, be devoted to them; to no others. Whatever good customs there are among us, they have to be adopted by you, not others.

(1, xi, 3)

Whatever Brāhmaṇas there may be who are superior to us, they should be comforted by you by giving them a seat. Gifts should be given with faith; should not be given without faith; should be given in plenty; should be given with modesty; should be given with fear, should be given with sympathy.

(I, xi, 4)

Then, if there is in you any doubt regarding rites and any doubt regarding conduct, you should conduct yourself in those cases in such a way in which those Brāhmaṇas who may be living there, who are competent to judge, dedicated (to good deeds), not led by others, not cruel and are lovers of virtue, conduct themselves in those cases.

(I, xi, 5)

Then in respect of persons who are accused (of sin), you should conduct yourself in such a way in which those Brāhmaṇas who may living there, who are competent to judge, dedicated (to good deeds), not led by others, not cruel and are lovers of virtue, conduct themselves in respect of such persons.

(I, xi, 6)

This is the command. This is the teaching. This is the secret meaning of the Vedas. This is the instruction. Thus should one worship; thus indeed should one worship this.

BRAHMĀNANDA VALLĪ

Here there is the Śānti which was given at the beginning of the Kaṭha-upaniṣad.

(II, i, 1)

The knower of Brahman attains the supreme. As to this, the following verse has been said :

He who knows Brahman as the real, as knowledge and as the infinite, placed in the cavity of the heart, in the highest heaven, realises all desires along with Brahman, the intelligent.

(II, ii, 1)

From food, verily, are produced whatsoever creatures dwell on the earth. Then by food alone, they live. And then into it also they pass at the end.

(II, iii, 1)

The gods breathe in pursuance of the life-breath; also men and beasts. Indeed, breath is the life of beings; therefore it is spoken of as the life of all.

(II, iv, 1)

Whence words return along with the mind, not attaining it—he who knows that bliss of Brahman fears not at any time.

(II, v, 1)

Understanding creates the sacrifice; rites also it creates. It is understanding that all the gods worship as Brahman, the greatest.

If one knows understanding as Brahman, and if he does not swerve therefrom, leaving the sins behind in his body, he enjoys all his desires.

(II, vi, 1)

He becomes non-existent if he knows Brahman as non-existent. If he knows that Brahman exists, then people know him as existent.

(II, vii, 1)

Non-existent verily, was this (world) in the beginning. Therefrom was, indeed, produced what is existent. That itself made its self. Therefore it is called well-made.

(II, viii, 1)

Here is an examination of (what is meant by) bliss. Let the student be a youth, a good youth, the best maintainer of discipline, most firm, most strong. To him this whole earth shall be filled with wealth. This one is the bliss of man. A hundred-fold of that bliss of man is the bliss of the human celestials.

This gradation of bliss is spoken of as increasing a hundred-fold with every next superior being until we come to Prajāpati and then to Brahman. Hence the section is called the Vallī dealing with the bliss of Brahman.

BHṚGU VALLĪ

(III, i, 1)

Bhṛgu, son of Varuṇa, approached his father Varuṇa with the request : Venerable sir, teach me Brahman. He explained to him this : food, vital breath, the eye, the ear, the mind, the word (as approaches to Brahman).

He (further) said to him : That, verily, from which these beings are born, that by which the beings live, that into which, when departing, they enter, seek to know that. That is Brahman.

(III, ii, 1)

He performed penance. After performing penance, he knew : Food is Brahman. Because, indeed, it is from food that these beings are born. The beings live by food. On departing, they enter food.

After knowing that, he once again approached Varuṇa, his father, with the request: Venerable sir, teach me Brahman. To him he explained: through penance seek to know Brahman. Penance is Brahman.

Then in three more successive stages of penance, he knew Brahman as life, as mind and as intellect. Each time he approached Varuṇa, he sent him back with the instruction to seek Brahman through further penance.

(III, vi, 1)

He again performed penance. After performing penance he knew: Brahman is bliss. Because, indeed, it is from bliss that these beings are born. The beings live by bliss. On departing they enter bliss.

This is the knowledge of Bhṛgu, son of Varuṇa, established in the highest heaven. Whoever knows this, becomes well established. He becomes endowed with food and becomes the eater of food. He becomes great in progeny, in cattle, in the lustre of spiritual knowledge, great in renown.

8

AITAREYA-UPANIṢAD

[*The Aitareya-upaniṣad belongs to the Rg-veda. It is divided into three chapters. It deals with the Self as the sole primary reality and describes the process of creation. It also teaches that through real knowledge, one gets away from the process of transmigration and attains immortality. The sage Vāmadeva is cited as an instance of one who has thus attained immortality.*]

PEACE CHANT

My speech is well established in my mind. My mind is well established in my speech. Increase again and again for me. Be a nail for my Veda. Do not abandon my learning. With this that has been studied, I maintain days and nights. I shall speak what is true. I shall speak what is real. Me may that protect. The speaker may that protect. May that protect me; may that protect the speaker. Om Peace, Peace, Peace.

(I, i, 1)

The self, verily, was in the beginning of this (world), the sole one. Nothing else whatsoever winked. He thought: Let me now create the worlds.

(I, i, 2)

He created these worlds: water, light-rays, death, the waters. This water is above the heaven. The heaven is its support. The light-rays are the interspace. Death is the earth. What are beneath, they are the waters.

(I, i, 3)

He thought: Here than are the worlds. Let me now create the guardians of the worlds. From the waters themselves, he drew forth a person, gave him a form.

(I, i, 4)

Over him he brooded. Of him who had been (thus) brooded over, the mouth burst forth, as if it were an egg. From the mouth (burst forth) speech; from speech Agni (fire). The two nostrils then burst forth. From the nostrils (burst forth) breath: from breath Vāyu (wind).

In this way the deities of the various phenomena of nature sprang forth from the different limbs of that person.

(I, ii, 1)

These various deities, created as above, fell into the great ocean. (Then the self) associated that (person) with hunger and thirst. Those (deities, being so associated with hunger and thirst), said to him (the creator) : Find out an abode for us, supporting ourselves wherein, we may take food.

(I, ii, 2)

For them, he brought a cow. They said : Indeed, this is not enough for us. For them, he brought a horse. They said: Indeed, this is not enough for us.

(II, ii, 3)

For them he brought a person. They said : This is well done, indeed, Person is what is well done. He said to them : You enter according to your proper abodes.

(II, ii, 4)

Agni, becoming speech, entered the mouth. Vāyu, becoming breath, entered the nostrils.

In this way the various deities transformed themselves into various sense-organs and functions and entered the person.

(I, ii, 5)

To him (the creator), hunger and thirst said: To us (also) find out (an abode). He said to them : I will locate you in these deities themselves. I will make you sharers with them.

(I, iii, 1)

Therefore, to whichever deity an offering is taken up, in that, hunger and thirst are really partakers of a share.

He (further) thought : Here are the worlds and the guardians of the worlds. Let me create food for them.

(I, iii, 2)

Over the waters he brooded. From them that had been (thus) brooded over, a form sprang forth. That which was born as that form is verily food.

(I, iii, 3)

This, created as above, desired to go outward. (The person) attempted to take hold of it with speech. He was not able to take hold of it with speech. If he had taken hold of it with speech, even with speech would one have had the satisfaction of food.

He attempted to take hold of food with the other functions like breath, but was not able to do so with any one of them.

(I, iii, 10)

Then he attempted to take hold of it with *apāna*. He got it. What is called *Vāyu* is he who takes hold of food. What is called *vāyu* is he who lives on food.

(I, iii, 11)

He thought: How can this (food) exist without me? He thought (again): Through which (door) shall I enter it? He (still again) thought: if speaking can be through speech, if breathing can be through breath, if meditation can be through mind, then who am I?

In the above passage there is reference to all the functions, though only a few are given here.

(I, iii, 12)

After opening that very end of the head, through that as door he entered it. That is that door which is called *vidṛti* (what is opened). This, as such, is *nandana* (what pleases). For that there are three abodes, three kinds of dreams as: this is the abode, this is the abode, this is the abode.

(I, iii, 13)

Being thus born, he perceived the created beings. What other thing does he talk about? He perceived this very person, Brahman, all-pervading. (He said): I have seen this.

(I, iii, 14)

Therefore his name is *idandra* (perceiver of this). Indeed, *indandra* is the name. Of Him, who is *idandra*, they speak indirectly as *indra*. Gods appear indeed to be fond of what is indirect.

A child has two births even before he is actually born; the first is in the state of the seed in the father and the seeond is when it enters the womb of the mother.

(II, i, 4)

He (the son) who is one self of his (father) is made his substitute (in this world) for the (performance of) meritorious deeds. Then the other self of his (father's), having done his duties, enters old age and departs. He, as soon as he departs from here, is born again. This is his (son's) third birth.

(II, i, 5)

This has been stated by the sage:

While I was in the womb, I knew all the births of the gods. A hundred fortresses made of steel guarded me. I have come down out of it with speed like a hawk.

Thus, Vāmadeva said this even when he was lying in the womb.

(II, i, 6)

He, knowing thus and springing upward, enjoyed, when this body was broken, all desires in that world of heaven, and became immortal, became (immortal).

(III, i, 1)

Who is this whom we worship as the self? Which of the two is that self? (Is it that) whereby one sees, or whereby one hears, or whereby one smells scents, or whereby one utters speech, or whereby one knows what is sweet and what is not sweet ?

Here various appellations of intelligence (prajñāna) are given, like heart, mind and consciousness. There are also given here various phenomena of nature starting from Brahmā and coming down to immovable objects.

(III, i, 3)

All this has intelligence as its eye and is established in intelligence. The world has intelligence as the eye. Intelligence is its support. Intelligence is Brahman.

(III, i, 4)

He (Vāmadeva), with this intelligent self, sprang forth from this world and having enjoyed all desires in that world of heaven, became immortal, became (immortal).

9

CHĀNDOGYA—UPANIṢAD

The Chāndogya-upaniṣad belongs to the Sāma-veda. It is a very long text. It begins with the identification of the music of the Sāma-veda with the highest reality. Then the entire Sāma-veda is identified with the highest reality. Later in this Upaniṣad appears the famous statement "That thou art" in which the individual self is identified with the supreme self. There are a large number of very interesting stories scattered throughout the text. The familiar Upaniṣadic teachings about Brahman as transcending the phenomenal world is presented in these stories. The most important portions in the Upaniṣad are where Ṣvetaketu receives the teaching of the identity of the individual with the Supreme from his father and where Sanatkumāra teaches that bliss is the highest reality.

The Śānti is the same as in the Kena.

THE UDGĪTHA AS BREATH

In the first section, there is the glorification of the Sāman singing, called Udgītha. This Udgīta is described as the essence of the Veda. This section deals mostly with the singing of Om and certain syllables which are used only for singing but which have no meaning.

(I, ii, 1)

When the gods and the demons, both of the race of Prajāpati, fought together, the gods took hold of the Udgītha, thinking: With this we shall overpower them.

(I, ii, 2)

They then worshipped the breath in the nose as the Udgītha. But the demons pierced it with sin. Therefore one smells both good odour and bad odour with it; because it was pierced with sin.

Then they worshipped the speech, the eye, the ear and the mind as the Udgītha with the same unsuccessful result.

(I, ii, 7)

Then they worshipped the breath in the mouth as the Udgītha. Hitting against it, the demons were destroyed, just as (a ball of earth) hitting against a solid piece of stone is destroyed.

Various sages worshipped that as the Udgītha.

(I, ii, 13)

Baka, son of Dalbha, knew it in that way. He became the Udgātā priest among those who resided in the Naimiśa (forest). He sang out all the desires for them.

THE UDGĪTHA AS ĀKĀŚA

The following anecdote gives an idea of the discussions on philosophical matters in ancient India.

(I, viii, 1)

There were three persons well versed in the Udgītha : Śilaka, son of Sālāvān, the son of Cikitāna of the Dalbha Gotra, and Pravāhaṇa, son of Jīvala. They said : We are indeed well versed in the Udgītha. Well, let us have a discussion about the Udgītha.

(I, viii, 2)

Assenting to it, they sat down. Then Pravāhaṇa, son of Jīvala, said : May you two worshipful ones first discuss. I will listen to the words of two Brāhmaṇas discussing.

(I, viii, 3)

Then Śilaka, son of Śālāvān, said to the son of Cikitāna of the Dalbha Gotra : Well, may I ask you ? He replied : Please ask.

(I, viii, 4)

He asked : What is the goal of the Sāmans ? He replied : It is the note.

Then he asked about the goal of notes and was told it is Prāṇa. But he could not stop there. Through successive questioning he learnt that food is the goal of Prāṇa, water the goal of food, and the heavenly world the goal of water. Beyond this the son of Cikitāna could not lead Śilaka.

(I, viii, 6)

Then Śilaka, son of Śālāvān, said to the son of Cikitāna of the Dalbha Gotra : You of

Dalbha Gotra, Sāman is not well established in you. If now someone were to say : your head will fall off, then your head would have fallen off.

(I, viii, 7)

He said : Well, I like to know this from you. He replied : Please know it.

He told him that this world is the goal of the heavenly world. The third disputant is not satisfied with this position and tells him that his head would fall off for his imperfect knowledge about Sāman. And he proposes to give the teaching he knows. He takes the goal further to Ākāśa and announces it as the knowledge imparted by Śaunaka to Śāṇḍilya.

THE STORY OF UṢASTI

The following is another interesting story :

(I, x, 1)

When the country of the Kurus was destroyed by thunder and hail, Uṣasti, son of Cakrāyaṇa, along with his very young wife, lived in a very miserable condition in the village of one who owned elephants (*i.e.*, who was very rich).

(I, x, 2)

He begged for food from the possessor of the elephants, who was eating beans. He said to him : I have nothing other than those which are now with me.

(I, x, 3)

Then he said : Please give me a part of these. He gave them to him. And then he said : Here is water to drink. He remarked : The leavings would be drunk by me (If I drink this water).

(I, x, 4)

He said : Are not these also leavings ? He replied : Indeed I shall not live if I do not eat them. And he added : I can get water to drink as I want.

(I, x, 5)

Having eaten them, he gave what remained to his wife. She had eaten well even before. After receiving them she kept them safe.

(I, x, 6)

In the morning on leaving (his bed), he said : Alas, if only I could get a little food, I can yet earn a little wealth. The king will be performing a sacrifice. He will choose me for all the priestly offices.

(I, x, 7)

To him the wife said : O my lord, here are those very beans. He ate those beans and went to that same sacrifice which was being performed.

(I, x, 8-9)

There he sat down near the Udgātā priests in the orchestra, who were to sing out. He said to the Prastotā priest : O Prastotā, that deity which belongs to your song, if you should sing without knowing that, your head will fall off.

He makes a similar statement to the other Udgātā priests.

(I, xi, 1)

Then to him the sacrificer said : I should like to know your honour. He replied : I am Uṣasti, the son of Cakrāyaṇa.

(I, xi, 2)

I desired to choose your honour for all these priestly offices. Since I could not secure your honour, I chose others. May your honour be pleased to make up all the priestly offices.

(I, xi, 3)

He said : Let it be so. Then he added : In that case with my permission let these very persons sing the praises. As much wealth you give to them, so much wealth you give to me also. The sacrificer said : let it be so.

The other priests asked him about the deities that belong to their respective songs and he replied that they are the Prāṇa, the sun and the food. He also told them that if they had sung without knowing the deities, their heads would have fallen off.

THE STORY OF JĀNAŚRUTI

In the following story persons who are rich in the worldly sense and who do public benefactions are held to be on a lower level in comparison with those who are rich in Brahman-knowledge and who are indifferent to worldly riches.

(IV, i, 1)

There lived (a king), a descendant of Janaśruta, his great-grandson, who gave gifts with faith, who gave gifts liberally, who arranged plenty of food cooked (for his guests). He got resting places built everywhere, thinking : They can eat my food everywhere.

(IV, i, 2)

One night some swans flew along. One of the swans said to another swan : Hei, Hei Bhallākṣa, Bhallākṣa, the lustre of the descendant of Janaśruta, his great-grandson, has spread through the sky alike. Do not come into contact with it; let it not burn you.

(IV, i, 3)

To him the other replied : O Kambara, you talk of him, who is only thus much, in the same way as of Raikva with the cart. The first asked : How is this Raikva with the cart ?

(IV, i, 4)

Just as (in gambling) all the lower figures belong to him who has the Kṛta which is the winning number, similarly whatever good things people do, they all come over to him. By me has been spoken thus he who knows what he knows.

(IV, i, 5)

The descendant of Janaśruta, his great-grandson, overheard this. He, as soon as he left his bed, spoke to his attendant : O friend, you talk (to me) in the same way as to Raikva with the chariot. (He asked :) How is this Raikva with the cart ?

(IV, i, 7)

The attendant searched for him and returned saying : I could not find him out. To him he said : O, where a Brāhmaṇa should be searched, there look for him.

(IV, i, 8)

He came to one who was scratching his itch underneath a cart. He asked him : Are you, your honour, Raikva with the chariot ? He replied : O, I am he.

The attendant returned saying : I have found him out.

(IV, ii, 1-2)

Then the descendant of Janaśruta, his great-grandson, went over to him, taking with him six hundred cows, an ornament and a chariot with mules. And he addressed him : O Raikva, here are six hundred cows. Here is an ornament. Here is a chariot with mules. Please teach me, your honour, that deity whom you worship.

(IV, ii, 3-4)

To him the other replied : Fie, fie, let the ornament and the chariot along with the cow be with you, O grief-blinded.

Then once again, the descendant of Janaśruta his great-grandson, went over to him, taking with him a thousand cows, an ornament, a chariot with mules and his daughter. He addressed him : O Raikva here are a thousand cows. Here is an ornament. Here is a chariot with mules. Here is a wife for you. Here is the village where you live. Please teach me.

(IV, ii, 5)

Lifting up her face, he said : O grief-blinded, you have brought these (to me). By this face alone are you able to make me speak.

These are the villages called Raikvaparṇas in the country of the Mahāvṛṣas where he lived.

Then he gave the teaching to the king.

THE STORY OF SATYAKĀMA

In the following story, faith and penance are shown as necesary antecedents of Brahman-knowledge.

(IV, iv, 1)

Satyakāma, the son of Jabalā, addressed his mother : Venerable lady, I desire to lead the life of a religious student. To what Gotra do I belong ?

(IV, iv, 2)

She said to him : O son, I do not know this, to what Gotra you belong. In my youth when I was moving about much and when I was a maid-servant, I obtained you. So I do not know to what Gotra you belong. I am Jabalā by name; and you are Satyakāma by name. Therefore you say that you are Satyakāma, son of Jabalā.

(IV, iv, 3)

He approached Gautama, son of Hari-drumata, and said : I desire to lead the life of a religious student under your honour. May I approach your honour ?

(IV, iv, 4)

To him he said : To which Gotra do you belong ? He said : I do not know this, to what Gotra I belong. I asked my mother. This is what she replied to me.

He gave the information he had received from his mother.

(IV, iv, 5)

To him he said: One who is not a Brāhmaṇa is not able to speak out like this. O beloved one, bring sacrificial fuel. I shall initiate you. You have not swerved from truth.

After initiating him, he brought out four hundred lean cows, bereft of strength and said: O beloved one, follow these.

Starting them, he said (again): Do not return without a thousand cows. He stayed away for a number of years, till the cows became a thousand.

(IV, v, 1)

Then to him a bull said: O Satyakāma. He replied: Your honour. He said: We have now become a thousand. Take us to the teacher's house. And I will explain to thee the parts of Brahman. He said: Your honour, please tell me.

The bull declared the four cardinal points as parts of Brahman. Then Fire declared to him earth, interspace, the heaven and the ocean as parts of Brahman. A swan declared to him fire, sun, moon and lightning as parts of Brahman. Lastly, a water-bird declared to him the Prāṇa, the eye, the ear and the mind as parts of Brahman.

(IV, ix, 1)

He reached the house of his teacher. To him the teacher said : O Satyakāma. He responded : O your honour.

(IV, ix, 2)

He said : O beloved one, you shine as though you knew Brahman. Who has taught it to you ? He replied : It is beings other than men. (He also added) : Your honour, it is my desire that you yourself should tell me (about Brahman).

(IV, ix, 3)

Indeed I have heard it said by persons like your honour : Knowledge can be the most efficient only if it is learned from a teacher. To him he said only this much : There is nothing here that is left out.

THE STORY OF UPAKOSALA

The following story explains the acquisition of Brahman knowledge in another way.

(IV, x, 1)

Upakosala, the son of Kamala, led the life of a religious student under Satyakāma, the son of Jabalā. He attended to his fires for twelve years. When he permitted the other disciples to return, he did not permit him alone to return.

(IV, x, 2)

To him his wife said: He has well attended to the fires as a religious student, with penance. Let not the fires blame you. Give him the teaching. But even without giving him the teaching, he went away.

(IV, x, 3)

Through grief he decided to fast. To him the teacher's wife said: O religious student, please eat. Why do you not eat?

He said: In this person there are many desires ungratified in different ways. I am filled with grief. I will not eat.

(IV, x, 4)

Then the fires said among themselves: This religious student has well attended to us with penance. Let us teach him.

The different fires taught him the identification of Brahman with various objects.

(IV, xiv, 1)

They said to him: O Upakosala, O beloved one, this is our knowledge, the knowledge of the self. The teacher will declare to you the path.

Then his teacher came. Him the teacher addressed: O Upakosala, he responded: Your honour.

(IV, xiv, 2)

(He said): O beloved one, your face looks that of one who knows Brahman. Who has taught you ? (He replied): Oh, who shall teach me ? Thus he, as it were, concealed the fact. Then he pointed out to the fires saying: Indeed, these of such nature have become of another nature.

(IV, xiv, 3)

(He asked): O beloved one, what indeed have they taught you ? He replied: This. Indeed, they have taught you about the worlds. But I will teach you that whereby sinful deeds do not cling to him who knows it thus, just as water does not stick on the leaf of a lotus.

(IV, xv, 1)

(He said): May your honour tell me that. To him he said: That person who is seen in the eye, he is the self. Thus he said. (He added): This is the immortal, the fearless. This is Brahman.

THE STORY OF ŚVETAKETU AND THE PAÑCĀLA KING

In the following story it is stated that the Kṣatriyas alone, and not the Brāhmaṇas, were the first custodians of the secret doctrine regarding the self.

(V, iii, 1)

Śvetaketu, the grandson of Aruṇa, went to the assembly of the Pāñcāla kingdom. Pravāhaṇa, son of Jivala, asked him : Boy, has your father taught you ? (He replied) : Yes, venerable sir.

He asked him some questions about death and after, and about return to life ; none of them he knew. So he said.

(V, iii, 4)

Then why did you say that you have been taught ? He who does not know these, how can he say he has been taught ?

Upset, he came to his father's home. He said to him : Your honour, even without teaching me you have told me 'I have taught you.'

(V, iii, 5)

That Kṣatriya merely by kin (not himself a true Kṣatriya) asked me five questions. I was not able to reply to even one of them. He replied : As you have not told me these, I do not know even one of them.

(V, iii, 6)

Then Gautama went to the place of the king. (The king said to him : O venerable Gautama, accept as boon any wealth which man possesses. He replied : O king, let the wealth which man possesses be yours, What word you have uttered in the presence of the boy, tell me that very word.

(V, iii, 7)

(The kịng) said to him : As you tell me O Gautama, this knowledge has not, before you, gone formerly to Brahmins. Therefore, this has remained the teaching of the Kṣatriyas among all.

Then the king teaches him about death and after. It is only knowledge that leads to final liberation. Those who lead a good life return after enjoyment in higher worlds.

THE STORY OF ŚVETAKETU AND HIS FATHER

In the following story Śvetaketu receives instruction from his father about reality and the creation of the world.

(VI, i, 1)

Śvetaketu was the grandson of Aruṇa. To him his father said : O Śvetaketu, live the life of a religious student. O beloved one, there was no one of our family who, without Vedic study, became as if a Brāhmaṇa by kin (not a true Brāhmaṇa himself).

(VI, i, 2-3)

He, who was twelve years old, approached (a teacher) and when he was twenty-four years old, he returned after studying all the Vedas.

To him his father said : O Śvetaketu, you are now conceited and struck up, considering yourself as learned in the Vedas. Have you asked for that instruction whereby what is not heard becomes heard, what is not thought about becomes thought about, and what is not known becomes known ? (The son asked) : O venerable sir, how can there be such an instruction ?

(VI, i, 4)

O beloved one, by one piece of clay all that is made of clay can be known. The modification is only a name depending on a word. The truth is that it is clay.

He gives further illustrations of the original and the modifications.

(VI, i, 7)

Those venerable persons, indeed, did not know this. If they had known this, why should they have not told me so ? He added : Your honour alone may tell me that.

(VI, ii, 1)

He said : Let it be so. O beloved one, in the beginning this was only as existence, one alone without a second. Here others say that in the beginning this was only as non-existence, one alone without a second. From that non-existence, existence was produced.

(VI, ii, 2-3)

He said : But O beloved one, how could this be so ? How could existence be produced from non-existence ? O beloved one, this was in the beginning only as existence, one alone without second. That (existence) thought : let me be born as many. That created light.

From the light was born water and from waters food. There is a description of the three-fold beings born of eggs, born of living beings (in the womb) and born of (roots by) sprouting. Then life entered all these beings.

In the sequel, Śvetaketu receives the great instruction from his father about the identity of the individual with the supreme in the statement, "That thou art." He teaches him first about sleep, about hunger and thirst. He says that the essence of all is the Self. Then the father teaches him this truth by apt illustrations.

(VI, ix, 1-2)

O beloved one, just as the bees make honey, they bring together into one essence the essences of trees situated in various places, and just as they (the essences) do not in that condition understand their distinction in the form, "I am the essence of this tree, I am the essence of this tree", in the very same way, indeed all these creatures attain the real and yet do not know that they have attained the real.

(VI, ix, 3)

Whatever they be here, a tiger, a wolf, a boar, a worm, a bird, a gnat or a mosquito, they become that again.

(VI, x, 1-2)

O beloved one, these rivers flow, the eastern to the east and the western to the west. From the ocean they reach even the ocean. They even become the ocean. Just as they do not know there, "I am this, I am this" in the same way O beloved one, all these creatures come from the real and yet do not know that they have come from the real.

(VI, xii, 1)

(The father): "Please bring a banyan berry." (The son): "Here, venerable sir." "Please cut it." "It is cut, venerable sir." "What do you see there?" "O venerable sir, these that look like small seeds." "Dear one, please cut one of these." "It is cut, venerable sir." "What do you see there?" "Nothing at all, venerable sir."

(VI, xii, 2)

To him (his father) said: Beloved one, this minute one which you do not see, it is, O beloved one, from this minute one that such a huge banyan tree springs forth. Listen to me with faith, O beloved one.

(VI, xii, 3)

That which is the subtle essence, all this is of the nature of that. That is truth, that is the self. That thou art, O Śvetaketu.

The individual dissolved in the absolute is compared to salt in water, which cannot be seen distinct as salt. The individual in ignorance, finding his way to the Supreme with the help of the teacher is compared to a man who, finding himself left blindfold in a wilderness, learns from someone the general direction of his native town and, asking people in village after village, finally reaches his home.

The next section deals with Bhūmavidyā (knowledge of the great). Bliss is declared as the highest.

THE STORY OF NĀRADA AND SANATKUMĀRA

(VII, i, 1)

Once Nārada approached Sanatkumāra saying : Venerable sir, please teach me. To him (Sanatkumāra) said : Come to me (first saying) that which you already know. Then I will tell you what is beyond that.

(VII, i, 2)

He said : I have studied the Ṛg-veda, the Yajur-veda and the Sāma-veda; the Atharva-veda as the fourth; Epics and Mythologies as the fifth; the Veda of the Vedas (Grammar); science of ancestral worship; mathematics; science of portents; science of time; logic; polity; etymology; subsidiary Vedic treatises like phonetics; science of spirits;

science of weapons; astronomy; science of snake-charming; fine arts. Venerable sir, I have studied all this. Venerable sir, I know merely the texts, not the self.

(VII, i, 3)

I have heard from persons like your honour that one who knows the self crosses sorrow. Here I am in sorrow. May your honour take me across to the other side of sorrow. To him he replied : All these things which you have studied, they are all only names.

(VII, i, 5)

(Sanatkumara said) : Meditate on name. (Narada asked) : Is there, venerable sir, anything higher than name ? (He replied) : Speech, indeed, is higher than name.

In this way he narrates higher and higher things, namely, mind, determination, intelligence, meditation, knowledge, strength, food, waters, light, ether, memory and hope. Then he continues :

(VII, xv, 1)

Life is higher than hope. Life indeed is all this.

A man who knows this and says so talks about transcendental things. But the one who really talks on the transcendental is the one who talks about the ultimate truth. Then Sanatkumāra leads Nārada through the knowledge of under-

standing, of thought, of faith, firm conduct, volition, and bliss to the ultimate truth.

(VII, xxiii, 1)

What is great is bliss. There is no bliss in the small. The great itself is bliss. The great itself is what is to be desired to be known.

Then there is a description of the great as that where one sees nothing else, hears nothing else and understands nothing else.

Sanatkumāra concludes the teaching of the Great thus :

(VII, xxvi, 2)

He who (really) sees no death, no illness nor even pain. He who (really) sees, sees everything and attains everything in every way.

Through purity of food results purity of intellect; through purity of intellect results steady memory; through the attainment of recollection all the knots are completely broken.

(In this way), crushing all his infirmities, Sanatkumāra showed him the other shore of darkness.

10

BṚHADĀRAṆYAKA-UPANIṢAD

[*The Bṛhadāraṇyaka-upaniṣad belongs to the Vājasaneyi School of the Yajur-veda. Like the Chāndogya, the text is a long one. It contains the highest teaching about Brahman as the one without a second. There is a good deal of miscellaneous matter that has not much interest or importance from the point of view of the main Upaniṣadic teaching. Maitreyī, the wife of Yājñavalkya, renounces all worldly possessions for the sake of knowledge that would lead her to immortality. Gārgi, another woman sage, puts highly philosophical questions to Yājñavalkya, when the latter challenged the assembly at the court of Janaka. The incidents are particularly interesting. The Śānti is the same as in Īśāvāsya-upaniṣad, The Upaniṣad begins with the glorification of the Aśvamedha sacrifice. There is a description of the process of creation and a statement of how sacrifice was created. In this connection there is the famous prayer for reality, light, and immortality.*)

From the unreal lead me to the real. From darkness lead me to light. From death lead me to immortality.

THE STORY OF GĀRGYA AND AJĀTAŚATRU

In this story, Ajātaśatru of Kāśī, a Kṣatriya gives the teaching of the self to Gārgya, a Brāhmaṇa, contrary to the natural order of Brāhmaṇas teaching the others.

(II, i, 1)

In the Gārgya family there was one named Dṛptabalāki who was very learned in the Vedas. He said to Ajātaśatru, king of Kāśi : I wish to speak to you about Brahman.

Ajātaśatru said : For this talk we will give you a thousand (cows). All people run about talking of Janaka and Janaka (alone).

(II, i, 2)

Gārgya (one belonging to the Garga family) said : That very person who is yonder in the sun, him indeed I worship as Brahman.

Ajātaśatru said : No, talk not to me about him. I worship him as the foremost, as the head of all creatures, as the king. He who worships him thus becomes foremost among all creatures, their head, their king.

Then Gārgya described Brahman as the Person in the moon, in the lightning, in space, in the wind, in fire, in water, in a mirror, as the sound which follows one when he goes, as the person in the quarters of heaven, as the person who consists of shadow. But Ajātaśatru silenced him on all points.

(II, i, 13)

Gārgya said : That very Person here in oneself, him indeed I worship as Brahman.

Ajātaśatru said : No, talk not to me about him. I worship him indeed as the one endowed with the self. He who worships him thus becomes endowed with the self. Indeed, his progeny will be endowed with the self.

(II, i, 14)

Gārgya became silent. Ajātaśatru said : Is this all ? (He replied) : Only this much. (The king said) : With this much, it is not known.

(II, i, 15)

Gārgya said : May I approach you (as a disciple). Ajātaśatru said : It is opposed to the natural order that a Brāhmaṇa should approach a Kṣatriya thinking, "He will teach me Brahman."

Indeed I will teach you : Thus saying, he took him by the hand and stood up. The two went up to a person who was sleeping. (The king) addressed him with the names : Great one, white-robed one, Soma, King. He did not get up. He pressed him with the hand and woke him up. Then he got up.

(II, i, 16)

Ajātaśatru said : When this man was asleep, that Person who consists of consciousness, where was he then ? Whence has he come now ? That even, Gārgya did not know.

(II, i, 17)

Ajātaśatru said : When this man was asleep, that Person who consists of consciousness, having by his consciousness taken up the consciousness of these senses, lies in that ether which is within the heart.

(II, i, 20)

As a spider goes out along the thread (it produces), and as from a fire small sparks go forth in all directions, even so from this self come forth all senses, all worlds, all gods, all beings. The secret name (Upaniṣad) thereof is 'the Real of the real.' The senses, verily, are real. Of them this (self) is the real.

YĀJÑAVALKYA AND MAITREYĪ

In this story, Maitreyī, wife of Yājñavalkya, spurns worldly possessions as not leading to immortality and receives from her husband the teaching about the highest truth that everything has a value not for itself but only in so far as it is the self, that when for one everything has become the self itself, there is no consciousness of knower and known, and that the self is the highest reality.

(II, iv, 1)

Yājñavalkya said : O Maitreyī, lo, I desire to leave off this state (of a householder).

Behold, let me make a final settlement for you and this Kātyayanī.

(II, iv, 2)

Maitreyī said : Sir, if this entire earth filled with wealth were mine, would I become immortal by that ?

Yājñavalkya said : No (you cannot). Just as is the life of men of means, so will your life be. There is no hope of immortality through wealth.

(II, iv, 3)

Maitreyī said : What shall I do with that through which I cannot become immortal ? Just what you know, Sir, that alone tell me.

(II, iv, 4)

Yājñavalkya said : Ah, dear as you are to us, dear is what you say. Come, sit down. I will explain to you. Attend well when I am explaining to you.

(II, iv, 5)

He said : Not indeed for the love of a husband is the husband dear. But, for the love of the self is the husband dear.

He makes similar statements about wife, sons, wealth, Brahminhood, Kṣatriyahood, the whole world, gods and creations.

Not indeed for the love of all is all dear. But, for the love of the self is all dear.

Lo, it is, indeed, the self that is to be seen, that is to be heard of, that is to be thought about, that is to be meditated on. Lo, Maitreyī, indeed by the sight of the self, by its being heard of, by its being thought about, by its being known, all this becomes known.

(II, iv, 6 & 12)

Everything will desert him who knows everything in aught other than the self. All this is this self. Arising out of these elements (the separateness of the self) disappears with them. After departing, there is no consciousness (of particularity). Thus said Yājñavalkya.

(II, iv, 13)

Maitreyī said : Just here you have confounded me, Sir, in saying : "After departing, there is no consciousness." Yājñavalkya said : Lo, I do not indeed say what confounds. Lo, enough, indeed, is this for understanding.

(II, iv, 14)

Where verily there is, as it were, a duality, there one knows another. Where indeed for one everything has become the self itself, there through whom and whom is one to know ? Him through whom one knows all this, through whom is one to know ? Lo, through whom one is to know the knower ?

(II, v, 1)

This earth is sweet as honey to all creatures. All creatures are like honey to this earth. And that person in this earth, who consists of light, who consists of immortality, that indeed is he who is that self. This is the immortal. This is Brahman. This is the All.

Then Yājñavalkya describes the Self through similar observations about waters, fire, wind, sun, quarters of heaven, moon, lightning, thunder, space, dharma, truth and mankind.

(II, v, 14)

This self is like honey to all creatures. All creatures are like honey to this self. And that Person in this self, who consists of light, who consists of immortality, that indeed is he who is that self. This is the immortal. This is Brahman. This is the All.

YĀJÑAVALKYA IN JANAKA'S COURT

In this story Yājñavalkya claims to be the most learned, takes challenge of all the Brāhmaṇas in the assembly of the Videha king, defeats them all in debate and vindicates his claim. Gārgī, a woman sage too participates in the debate.

(III, i, 1)

Janaka, king of the Videhas, performed a sacrifice where many presents were given away.

There Brāhmaṇas had assembled from the Kingdom of the Kurupāñcālas.

In this Janaka, king of the Videhas, there arose a desire to know : who among these Brāhmaṇas may be the most learned in the Vedas ? He brought together a thousand cows. There were ten gold coins tied to the horns of each.

(III, i, 2)

He said to them : O Venerable Brāhmaṇas, he who among you is the best established in the knowledge of Brahman, can drive these cows (home). Those Brāhmaṇas could not make up their minds.

Then Yājñavalkya said to his own disciple : O beloved Sāmaśravas, drive on these (cows). He drove them on.

Those Brāhmaṇas became angry. (They said) : How can he declare himself as the best established among us in the knowledge of Brahman ?

Now there was Hotā priest of Janaka, king of the Videhas, named Aśvala. He asked him : Are you, Yājñavalkya, the best established among us in the knowledge of Brahman ?

He said : We do obeisance to him who may be the best established in the knowledge of Brahman. We are only desirous of the cows.

(III, i, 3)

The Hotā priest Aśvala made up his mind to question him even there. He said : O Yājñavalkya, when everything here is overtaken by death, by what means can the sacrificer overcome the approach of death ?

Yājñavalkya replies that it is by the Hotā priest. Then Aśvala questions about various changes and destructions in the world like day and night, the waxing and the waning of the moon; and Yājñavalkya explains the means for overcoming each of them. Asked about the number of chants that the Udgātā priest had to sing that day in the sacrifice, Yājñavalkya replied that the chants were three, and explained their fruit.

(III, i, 10)

One attains only the earthly world through the introductory chant, the interspace through the accompanying chant and the heavenly world through the benediction chant.

Thereupon Aśvala, the Hotā priest, withdrew.

(III, ii, 1)

Then Ārtabhāga of Jaratkaru gotra questioned. He said : Yājñavalkya, how many are the *grahas* (senses) and how many are the *atigrahas* (their functions) ?

Yājñavalkya replies that there are eight grahas : breath, speech, tongue, eye, ear, mind, hands and skin; and eight atigrahas : apāna (odour), name, taste, form, sound, desire, action, and touch. Then there is the question :—

(III, ii, 12)

He said : O Yājñavalkya, when a man dies, what is it that does not leave him ? (He replied) : It is name. Indeed, name is endless. Through that he attains even the endless world.

(III, ii, 13)

He said : O Yājñavalkya, when of a dead man the breath goes into the air, the soul into ether, where then is this person ?

(Yājñavalkya said) : Give me your hand, beloved Ārtabhāga. Let us two alone know about this. We shall not (talk of) this where there are people. Thus they two departed and discussed about it in secret.

Thereupon Ārtabhāga of Jaratkaru gotra withdrew.

(II, iv, 1)

The Uṣasta, son of Cakra, questioned. He said : O Yājñavalkya, the Brahman that is directly seen and not beyond one's view, the self that is within all, explain to me that.

"It is that self of yours that is within all." "Which one, O Yājñavalkya, that is within all ?" "He who breathes with your life-breath, that is the self of yours that is within all."

(III, iv, 2)

Then Uṣasta, son of Cakra, said : Just as one can say : "This is a cow, this is a horse," so has this been explained. That very Brahman that is directly seen and not beyond view, that self that is within all, explain to me that.

You cannot see the seer of seeing. You cannot know the knower of knowing. This is that self of yours which is within all. Whatever is other than this is mutable.

Thereupon Uṣasta, son of Cakra, withdrew.

(III, vi, 1)

Then Gārgī, the daughter of Vacaknu, questioned (him). She said : O Yājñavalkya, since all this is woven warp and woof on water, on what is water woven warp and woof ?

He replies that it is on wind. The wind is woven on inter-space. And then came in succession the worlds of the Gandharvas, of the sun, moon, stars, gods, Indra and Prajāpati and at last the world Brahmā. Each earlier world is said to be woven on the subsequent one.

(She asked); On what is the world of Brahmā woven warp and woof ? He said : O Gārgī do not ask questions about the transcendental. You are asking transcendental questions about the deity about whom such transcendental questions should not be asked.

Thereupon Gārgī, daughter of Vacaknu, withdrew.

After a series of questions by another about the inner controller, to which Yājñavalkya answers saying that the immortal self within all is the inner controller, Gārgī re-appears.

(III, viii, 1)

Then (Gārgī), the daugher of Vacaknu, said : Venerable Brāhmaṇas, behold, I will put him two questions. If he is able to answer me those (questions), then never can any one among you defeat him in discussion about Brahman.

(III, viii, 2)

(They said) : O Gārgī, ask. She said : O Yājñavalkya, just as a citizen of Kāśī or the King of Videha, a youth of heroic ancestry, after stringing his bow from which the string had been taken off, and taking in his hand two arrows that can pierce through the enemy, may go up to his enemy, in the same way will I approach you with two questions. Answer me these two questions. (Yājñavalkya said) : O Gārgī, ask.

Then she asks him across what is that woven warp and woof—that which is above the sky, that which is beneath the earth, that which is between these two, that which is past, present and future.

Yājñavalkya says that it is woven across space. Then she asks him across what space is so woven.

(III, viii, 8)

He said : O Gārgī, Brāhmaṇas call that, indeed, the immutable, what is not gross, what is not subtle. He who without knowing this immutable performs sacrifices in this world, that remains limited alone for him.

(III, viii, 10)

But he who, knowing this immutable, departs from this world becomes a Brāhmaṇa.

(III, viii, 11)

That immutable, verily, O Gārgī, is the unseen seer, the unheard hearer, the unthought thinker, the ununderstood understander. Other than it there is nothing that sees. Other than it there is nothing that thinks. Other than it there is nothing that understands. Across this immutable, verily, O Gārgī, is space woven, warp and woof.

Thereupon she withdrew. Another asked him many questions about gods and their relations to Brahman. Yājñavalkya answered all the questions to the satisfaction of the assembly; and all withdrew from the discussion.

(III, ix, 27)

Then he said : Venerable Brāhmaṇa whoever among you desires, let him ask me. Or let all of you ask me. Whoever among you desires (to be questioned) let me ask him Or let me ask all of you.

Those Brāhmaṇas could not make up their minds.

YĀJÑAVALKYA'S INSTRUCTIONS TO JANAKA

In this story Yājñavalkya gives the teaching of the highest to King Janaka through successive stages and refuses to accept a present until the real teaching is imparted. He teaches that the soul is to be known as not this, not that. He also gives the teaching about the nature of transmigration.

(IV, i, 1)

The king of the Videhas named Janaka was sitting (on his throne). Once Yājñavalkya went (to him). To him (the king) said : O Yājña-valkya, for what purpose have you come ? Is it desiring cows or desiring (disputations) culminating in subtle points ? (Yājñavalkya) replied : Your majesty, both.

(IV, i, 2)

(Yājñavalkya continued) : What anybody may have told you, let me hear that. The king said : Jitvā, son of Śilina, (told) me : "Speech indeed, is Brahman."

Just as one can say that he has a mother and a father, so has the son of Śilina told you. Did he tell you about its seat and support ?

(The king said) : He did not tell me (that). (Yājñavalkya said) : Your Majesty, this is verily an one-legged (Brahman). (The king said) : O Yājñavalkya, tell us (about that.)

Yājñavalkya said that its seat is speech and its support ether. Then—

Janaka, king of the Videhas, said : I will give you a thousand cows with a bull as large as an elephant. Yājñavalkya said : My father was of opinion that one should not accept without first teaching.

As desired by Yājñavalkya before giving him the true teaching about Brahman, the king tells him what he has heard from five others. In each case Yājñavalkya establishes that Brahman known in those ways is only an one-footed Brahman. At the end of each explanation, the king offers Yājñavalkya a thousand cows as before, and at every time Yājñavalkya refuses to accept the gift before giving him the true teaching.

(IV, ii, 1)

Janaka, king of the Videhas, came down from his seat and said : O Yājñavalkya, let salutation be to you. Give me the teaching.

He replied : Your Majesty, verily, just as one desiring to go a long way arranges for a chariot or a boat, in the same way you have provided yourself with these Upaniṣadic teachings. Thus being in the company of gods, high-born, having studied the Vedas, with the Upaniṣads expounded to you, whither will you go when you are released hence?

(The king said): Venerable Sir, that I do not know—whither I shall go. (Yājñavalkya said): Now I shall tell you that—whither you will go. (The king said); Venerable Sir, tell me.

Then Yājñavalkya begins to teach the king the true nature of Brahman and says:

(IV, ii, 4)

That self is not this, it is not that. It is not grasped, being ungraspable. It is not injured. Verily, Janaka, you have reached (the stage of) fearlessness. Thus spoke Yājñavalkya.

Janaka, king of the Videhas, said: O Yājñavalkya, let fearlessness come to you who, venerable Sir, teach us fearlessness. Let salutation be to you. Here is the Videha kingdom. Here I am.

The following is the account of another meeting between Janaka and Yājñavalkya when the latter discourses on Brahman and explains the nature of transmigration.

(IV, iii, 1)

Yājñavalkya went to Janaka, king of the Videhas. He decided: I shall not discourse.

But then, when Janaka king of the Videhas, and Yājñavalkya had (once before) had a discussion at an Agnihotra, Yājñavalkya had offered him a boon. He chose (as the boon) liberty to ask any question he desired. And to him (Yājñavalkya) had given that boon.

(IV, iii, 2)

Him the emperor himself asked first: O Yājñavalkya, of what light is this Person? He replied: Of solar light, your Majesty. By the solar light alone he sits, he moves around, he does deeds, he returns.

(IV, iii, 3)

(The king said): O Yājñavalkya, it is even so. When the sun sets, O Yājñavalkya, of what light is this very Person?

Yājñavalkya says that it is lunar light. In the absence of both, it is the light of fire. Then Yājñavalkya proceeds through the light of speech to the light of the self.

(IV, iii, 6)

(Yājñavalkya said): The self alone becomes his light. With the light of the self alone he sits, he moves around, he does deeds, he returns.

In detail, Yājñavalkya explains the conditions of the self, namely, dream state and deep sleep.

(IV, iii, 32)

Your Majesty, he whose world is Brahman becomes an ocean, the one seer, free from duality. This is his highest path. This is his highest world. This is his highest bliss.

(IV, iii, 33)

(The king said) : I will give you a thousand cows. Speak beyond this even for my release. At this Yājnavalkya was afraid : This king who is intelligent has driven me from all corners.

(IV, iv, 3)

Now, as a caterpillar comes to the end of a grass-blade and closes itself in taking the next jump, in the very same way, the self destroys this body, drives away nescience and closes itself in taking the next jump.

(IV, iv, 4)

Now, as a goldsmith, taking a piece of gold, makes another, newer and more beautiful form, in the very same way, the self destroys this body, drives away nescience and makes another newer and more beautiful form.

(IV, iv, 7)

As the slough of a snake lies on an ant-hill being cast off there, in the very same way lies this body. Then this incorporeal immortal Life is indeed Brahman, indeed light.

(IV, iv, 25)

Verily the great self is the unborn, unaging, undying, immortal, fearless Brahmau. Verily Brahman is fearlessness. He who knows thus becomes Brahman that is fearlessness.

11

ŚVETĀŚVATARA-UPANIṢAD

[The Śvetāśvatara-upaniṣad belongs to the Taittirīya School of the Yajur-veda. Though not included in the ten major Upaniṣads, it is regarded as an ancient and important Upaniṣad. In this, God in the form of Rudra is spoken of as the highest Deity, from whom as cause, both material and efficient, the world has evolved and who protects and controls the world. He is identified with the supreme Brahman. The Upaniṣad derives its name from the sage who taught the truth contained in it. In the order of the 108 Upaniṣads this bears the number 14. The Śānti is the same as in Kaṭha-upaniṣad.]

(i, 1)

Those who discourse on Brahman say :

What is the cause ? Brahman ? Whence are we born ? Whereby do we live ? And wherein are we established ? Presided over by whom do we, O knowers of Brahman, live our different conditions in pleasures and pains ?

(i, 2)

Time, nature, necessity, chance, the elements, the womb, or the person : these are to be considered (as the cause). It is not a combination of these, because of the existence of the self. Even the self is powerless in respect of the cause of pleasure and pain.

(i, 3)

They who follow the Yoga of meditation saw the divine self-power hidden in its own qualities. It is that one who presides over all the causes from time to the soul.

(i, 8)

The Lord supports this all which is a combination of the mutable and the immutable, of the manifest and the unmanifest. And the self being powerless, is bound on account of his being the enjoyer. Knowing God, he is released from all fetters.

(i, 9)

There are two unborn ones : the knowing (God) and the unknowing (soul), the powerful and the powerless. Indeed there is (another) one who (too) is unborn and is connected with the enjoyer and the objects of enjoyment. The self is infinite, of cosmic form, and non-active. When one attains this triad, that is Brahman.

(ii, 5)

I join your ancient prayers with adorations. My verses go forth as suns in their path. All the sons of the immortal listen, they who have ascended to the divine abodes.

(ii, 14)

As a mirror lustrous by nature, but stained by dust, shines when it is cleaned, so the embodied one, on seeing clearly the real nature of the self, becomes one, with his purpose achieved and freed from sorrow.

(ii, 15)

When one having attained to Yoga sees clearly the real nature of Brahman through the real nature of the self which can be compared to a lamp, then, knowing God, the unborn, steadfast, free from every nature, one is released from all fetters.

(iii, 2)

Indeed, Rudra is the one—they do not stand for second—who lords over these worlds with his lordly powers. He stands opposite the men; after creating all the worlds he, the protector, merges them together at the end of time.

(iii, 4)

He who is the beginning and source of the gods, who is greater than all, Rudra, the great seer, who of old created the Hiraṇyagarbha, may He endow us with propitious intellect.

(iii, 5)

That body of yours, O Rudra, which is auspicious, unterrific, showing no evil, with that most benign body manifest yourself to us, O dweller in the mountains.

(iii, 6)

That arrow, O dweller in the mountains, which you hold in your hands to throw, make that benign, O protector of the mountain; do not injure man or beast.

(iv, 1)

The One who himself without a colour, by the manifold wielding of his power, gives manifold colours with a concealed purpose and (into whom) in the beginning and in the end the universe dissolves, He is the god. May he endow us with propitious intellect.

(iv, 2)

That is itself Fire; that is the sun; that is Air; and that is the moon; that itself is the bright. That is Brahman; that is water; that is Prajāpati.

(iv, 3)

You are woman; you are man; you are the youth and also the maiden; you as an old man totter with a stick; being born, you become facing all directions.

(iv, 5)

The One, unborn, red, white and black, who produces manifold offspring similar in form to herself; there lies the one male, unborn, delighting; another male, unborn, leaves her off after having had his enjoyment with her.

(iv, 9)

The Vedas, the sacrifices, the rituals, the observances, the past, the future, and whatever the Vedas declare—this universe that illusion-maker projects from that (Brahman). And the other (the soul) is confined within that (the world) by illusion.

(iv, 10)

Now, know Prakṛti as Māyā and the Great Lord as the wielder of Māyā. This entire world is pervaded by what form His limbs.

(iv, 20)

His form is not capable of being seen. With the eye no one sees Him. They who know Him thus with the heart, with the mind, as abiding in the heart, become immortal.

(v, 12)

Gross and subtle, and even innumerable forms, the soul takes on according to his qualities. Every succeeding cause of his association with them is to be seen through the qualities of his actions and of himself.

(vi, 1)

Some sages speak of the nature (as the cause). Others, badly deluded, speak similarly of time. But it is the greatness of God whereby this wheel of Brahmā is being turned.

(vi, 4)

Starting with works that are associated with qualities, he who will distribute all the existents (he is the real Yogin). In the absence of those existents, there is the destruction of the deeds already done. And when deeds are destroyed, he becomes really quite another.

(vi, 11)

He, is the one God, hidden in all beings, pervading all, the inner self of all, the perceiver of all deeds, the presider of all beings, the witness, the knower, the sole one, and devoid of qualities.

(vi, 18)

He who of old created Brahmā, and who verily imparted the Vedas to him, that god who manifests in his own intellect, I, in my eagerness for release, approach as a refuge.

(vi, 21)

By the power of his penances and through the grace of God, Śvetāsvatara, the wise, spoke about Brahman, the supreme, the pure, pleasing to the company of seers, in the proper way for the sake of the ascetic order.

12

KAUṢĪTAKĪ-UPANIṢAD

[*The Kauṣītakī-upaniṣad belongs to the Ṛg-veda. It is not included in the ten major Upaniṣads ; yet it is an important one. It deals with the usual Upaniṣadic problem of the absolute transcending the phenomenal world, identifies Prāṇa with the highest Truth and extols the knower of the Truth. Among the 108 Upaniṣads, it occupies the 25th place. The Śānti is the same as in Aitareya-upaniṣad.*]

(i, 1)

Citra, grandson of Garga, desiring to perform a sacrifice, chose Āruṇi (as the officiating priest). He sent his son Śvetaketu saying : you conduct the sacrifice.

When he was seated (as the officiating priest), (Citra) asked : Son of Gautama, is there a place concealed in the world in which you will put me ? Or is there another path ? Will you put me in its world ?

He replied : I do not know this. However, I will ask my Teacher. He went to his father and asked : He spoke to me thus. How am I to reply ?

He replied : I too do not know this. Even in that assembly we will learn the Veda and receive what our betters give. Come. Let us both go.

With sacrificial fuel in hand he went to Citra, grandson of Garga (and said) : I approach you (to receive the teaching). To him he replied : You are worthy of Brahman-knowledge, O Gautama, since you have approached me. Come, I will teach you.

He then explained how one goes to the world of the moon; and then if he is a knower, he goes beyond to the Devayāna and if he does not know, he is dropped back. Along the Devayāna, the knower goes to the various higher worlds till he reaches the world of Brahmā. There he makes triumphal progress.

(i, 4)

Five hundred celestial nymphs approach him, one hundred with garlands in their hands, one hundred with ointments in their hands, one hundred with powders in their hands, one hundred with garments in their hands and one hundred with fruits in their hands. Him they adorn with the ornaments of Brahman. Having been adorned with the ornaments of Brahman, he, the knower of Brahman, proceeds to Brahman.

In the following section Prāṇa is described as identical with Brahman, the highest Truth. All divinities pay homage to him without his having to ask for anything and so do all beings. To him who knows Prāṇa as Brahman also, all divinities and all beings pay similar homage.

(ii, 1)

Kauṣītakī was wont to say : Prāṇa is Brahman. To this same Prāṇa as Brahman, verily, all these gods bring offering without his begging. Indeed in the same way, to him all beings bring offering without his begging.

Of him who knows thus, there is the secret doctrine : One shall not beg. It is as if, having begged in a village and not having received anything, one were to sit down (and say) : I shall not eat what is given here.

Those very persons who first refused him would invite him (saying) : Let us give to you.

This the virtue of the non-beggar. One or other would invite him saying : Let us give to you.

In the following section Indra gives the teaching of his own identity with the highest Truth and extols the person who knows him thus :

(iii, 1)

Pratardana, son of Divodāsa, went to the favourite abode of Indra through fighting and valour. To him Indra said : O Pratardana, I will give you a boon.

Then Pratardana said : You yourself choose (for me) what you consider to be the most beneficial to a man. To him Indra said : Indeed one does not choose a boon for another. You yourself must choose.

Then there shall be no boon for me : thus said Pratardana. Thereupon Indra went to him as the Deity of Truth. Indra is indeed Truth.

Then he said : Know me alone. This itself I consider what it most beneficial to a man, that he should know me.

He who should know me, for him this world is not injured by any of his deeds, not by the killing of his mother, not by the killing of his father, not by stealing, not by the killing of an embryo.

(iii, 2)

He said (again) : I am Prāṇa of the nature of knowledge. Me of that nature worship as life immortal. Indeed as long as Prāṇa abides in this body, so long does (also) life. Indeed through Prāṇa alone does one attain immortality in this world.

(iii, 8)

Desire not to know speech; one shall know the speaker. Desire not to know smell; know him who smells. Desire not to know colour; know him who understands colour.

Thus there is the statement about all the senses of cognition and of action.

These ten subtle elements of being alone there are with reference of intelligence; and ten subtle elements of intelligence there are with reference to beings. If there be no subtle elements of being, there would be no subtle elements of intelligence. If there be no subtle elements of intelligence, there would be no subtle elements of being.

13

SĀMĀNYAVEDĀNTA-UPANIṢADS

There are twenty-four Minor Upaniṣads which deal with the general Upaniṣadic doctrine that Brahman is the only supreme reality, whence the phenomenal world appears. Release from the bonds of the world is the goal of man. It can be attained even in life. Knowledge is what leads to this release. Of the twenty-four Upaniṣads, selections from the Kauṣītakī have already been given.

The number of the Upaniṣad in the order of the 108 is also given along with the reference number. The Upaniṣads are arranged in the order of the Sanskrit alphabet. The Śānti is not given separately for each of the Upaniṣads, since that can be known by a reference to the Veda to which it is assigned.

AKṢĪ-UPANIṢAD

YAJURVEDA—TAITTIRĪYA

In this the Sun God imparts the teaching of Brahman to Śāṅkṛti. The various stages of Yoga leading to final realisation are described here.

(72. i, 1)

Then the venerable Śaṅkṛti went to the world of the Sun. Bowing to the Sun, he worshipped him through the Cākṣuṣmatī Vidyā (learning about the eyes).

Nārāyaṇa in the form of the sun was very much pleased with being worshipped through Cākṣuṣmatī Vidyā, and said : In the family of the Brāhmaṇa who studies every day the Cākṣuṣmatī Vidyā no one will be blind; there will be the acquisition of learning.

ADHYĀTMA-UPANIṢAD

YAJURVEDA—VĀJASANEYĪ

Here Nārāyaṇa is identified with the highest being. Superimposition of the phenomenal world on the reality, its removal, release in life and final release are described here.

(73. 12)

By the cessation of deeds there will be the cessation of desires. Thence the destruction of residual impressions. The destruction of impressions is final release. This (release) is admitted to be release in life.

ANNPŪRṆA-UPANIṢAD

ATHARVA-VEDA

In this, on the request of a seeker after truth named Nidāgha, the sage Ribhu who knows Brahman describes how he propitiated the goddess

Annapūrṇā, and learned the truth about Brahman through Her grace. The nature of bondage and release is also dealt with.

(70. i, 20)

Whatsoever here is seen, regard that as non-existent. just like the city of the Gandharvas, just like the water in a mirage.

(70. iv, 14)

There are two kinds of cessation of mental functions, that which has a form and that which has no form. At the stage of release in life, it has a form; what pertains to release from body is devoid of form.

ĀTMĀ-UPANIṢAD

ATHARVA-VEDA

Here the three-fold nature of the self, as the individual, the immanent and the supreme, is dealt with.

(76. 22-23)

Just as when a jar is broken, ether becomes ether alone, similarly when the adjuncts are dissolved, one who knows Brahman becomes Brahman itself.

ĀTMAPRABODHA-UPANIṢAD

ṚG-VEDA

It starts with a glorification of the mantra "Om namo Nārāyaṇāya" of eight syllables. The identity of the inner self with Brahman, knowledge as means for release and the best and the middling in respect of those who are eligible for study are dealt with here.

(41. 28-29)

The flame of a lamp, though small, destroys immense darkness. Similarly, knowledge, though small, will destroy the great ignorance.

EKĀKṢARA-UPANIṢAD

YAJUR-VEDA—TAITTIRĪYA

There is here a glorification of Nārāyaṇa as of the nature of the all.

(61. 6)

The first creator, the creator of the manifold universe, the air, the swan, Viṣṇu, the Boar, night, solitude, what is created, what will be created, creation, the deeds, time, order and the supreme immutable—all these are yourself.

GARBHA-UPANIṢAD

YAJUR-VEDA—TAITTIRĪYA

This gives an elaborate description of the constituents of the body. The soul abides in it and longs for liberation.

(17. 1)

Of five-fold form, abiding in the five (elements), depending upon the six (tastes), having association with the six qualities, of seven elements, of three impurities, of two origins, made of the four kinds of food—such is the body.

NIRĀLAMBANA-UPANIṢAD

YAJUR-VEDA—VĀJASANEYĪ

Here there is a description of forty-one topics: Brahman, god, the various divinities and celestials and various aspects of life here and hereafter, ending with the description of a Samnyāsin.

(34. 4)

What is called the Lord is Brahman itself. Relying on his own power which is designated Prakṛti, he created the universe and entered it as the immanent. He controls the intellect, the senses, etc. So he is the Lord of Brahmā and others.

(34. 39)

Casting off all Dharmas, becoming free from egoity and selfishness, approaching the longed for Brahman as the refuge, deciding "I am Brahman itself" through meditation free from mental processes, thus goes about the Yati absolute lord of himself. He is the Samnyāsin. He is the liberated. He is the one to be worshipped. He is the Yogin. He is the Paramahamsa. He is the Avadhūta (one who has shaken off everything).

PAIṄGALA-UPANIṢAD

YAJUR-VEDA—VĀJASANEYĪ

Here Yājñvalkya imparts to Paiṅgala, at the latter's request, the supreme teaching about final release. The process of creation, how the Lord became an individual soul, the explanation of the Mahāvākyas, the nature of a knower—these are the various main topics dealt with.

(51. i, 12)

The omniscient Lord, as associated with a little of Māyā, entered the individual body, and being deluded by her (Māyā) became the soul. Due to identification with the three-fold body, he became doer and enjoyer.

PRĀṆĀGNIHOTRA-UPANIṢAD

YAJUR-VEDA—TAITTIRĪYA

Here there is a description of Prāṇa as identical with the highest reality : dedication of the self and the body for purposes of mental purification is also prescribed as a necessary preliminary to release.

(14. 14)

The Prāṇa, the Fire, is the supreme Self, associated with the five vital breaths. (Through) him) let me have fearlessness from all beings; let there be no fear for me at any time.

(14. 15)

You are as Vaiśvānara Fire, the all. All forms that are born are maintained by you. All the oblations are the all, in which you are the immortal Brahman.

MANTRIKĀ-UPANIṢAD

YAJUR-VEDA—VĀJASANEYĪ

Here the nature of the highest Brahman, its apparent entanglement in Māyā, the distinctive nature of the individual and the supreme Brahman, the manifestation of Brahman as various phenomena and release through knowledge are described.

(32. 3-4)

The producer of changes, the insentient, of eight-fold form, unborn, steadfast, thus he who makes the super-imposition contemplates (Māyā). Through this, he is entangled and again impelled. The goal of man is worked out. By him (who makes the super-imposition) is this world presided over.

MAHĀ-UPANIṢAD

SĀMA-VEDA

This is a very long Upaniṣad and contains detailed descriptions of the world and release from it. Nārāyaṇa is spoken of as the highest Being. The manifest world and gods like Rudra and Brahmā are born of him.

(61. iv, 66)

Indeed, the mind, as tainted by afflictions like desire, alone is transmigratory life. The same, when freed therefrom, is spoken of as the end of transmigration.

(61. iv, 67)

He who is fit to assume a body becomes embodied, being thought of thus by the mind. When he is freed from the impressions of the body, he is not tainted by the attributes of the body.

(61. v, 52)

At first the mind arose from reality, the supreme Self. By that, was spread out this world, aggregate of attributes, O intelligent one, just as the non-existent blue colour which is spoken of as the most beautiful, is (manifested) by the non-existent sky.

(61. v, 53)

When the mind is dissolved on account of the destruction of the attributes, the mists of worldly delusions also disappear. Like the sky on the approach of summer, pure intelligence, the one, the unborn, the first, the endless, shines clear within.

MUKTIKĀ-UPANIṢAD

YAJUR-VEDA—VĀJASANEYĪ

Here Śrī Rāma explains to Hanumān how a study of the Upaniṣads leads to release; incidentally he enumerates the 108 Upaniṣads, the method of their study and the Śānti for the various Upaniṣads. The destruction of impressions, samādhi, and dedication to the Lord are also dealt with.

(108. i, 26)

This release of complete isolation, by what means is it to be attained? Even the one Māṇḍūkya is enough for the release of those who desire release.

(108. i, 27)

If even then knowledge is not attained, you must learn the ten Upaniṣads. Acquiring knowledge, without any lapse of time, you will reach the abode that belongs to me (Rāma, the Lord).

(108. i, 28-29)

If even then, O Hanumān (son of Añjanā), there is no steadfastness in the knowledge, learn the thirty-two Upaniṣads and stop. If your longing is for release with freedom from the body, you must learn the one hundred and eight Upaniṣads.

MUDGALA-UPANIṢAD

SĀMA-VEDA

Nārāyaṇa is spoken of as the highest reality. Brahman itself becomes the individual soul through association with the three-fold miseries in life.

(57. ii, 3)

Nārāyaṇa, the Puruṣa, is what has been, what is yet to be, and what will be. And He of that nature became the giver of release to all. And He is greater than all that is great. To Him none is superior.

(57. iii, 1; iv, 1)

The one god, settling himself in various forms, being unborn, is born in various ways. That is Brahman, transcending the three-fold miseries, free from the six sheaths, devoid of the six modes of existence and distinct from all that can be designated as "thus."

MAITRĀYANĪ-UPANIṢAD

SĀMA-VEDA

Here a sage Śākāyanya imparts to the King Bṛhadratha, who retired to the forest finding no peace in life, the teaching of the highest reality, after offering him lesser things which the king rejects.

(24. iv, 2)

Through penance is attained pure being. From pure being is attained mind. Through mind is attained the self. Through the attainment of the self (the world) recedes.

(24. iv, 9)

That happiness which one attains for the mind that has been cleansed of all impurities by meditation and that is put at rest on the self, it is not possible for one to describe in words. At that time it is grasped by the internal organ by itself.

VAJRASŪCIKĀ-UPANIṢAD

SĀMA-VEDA

Here a Brāhmaṇa is described not as a particular individual self nor as a particular body, nor knowledge nor virtue nor any such thing, but as one who has realised Brahman.

(36. 6, 8)

Even among Kṣatriyas and others there are many who have seen the Truth and who are real knowers. Therefore knowledge is not what characterises a Brāhmaṇa. Among Kṣatriyas and others there are many who are givers of gold. Therefore a virtuous man need not be a Brāhmaṇa.

(36. 9)

Then who is it that is called a Brāhmaṇa ? Anyone who has been able to directly perceive the self without a second, as (clearly as one can see) the *āmalaka* fruit held on the palm, is a Brāhmaṇa.

ŚĀRĪRAKA-UPANIṢAD

YAJUR-VEDA—TAITTIRĪYA

Here the ten sense organs are described as forms of the five elements. The four internal organs, the three Guṇas and their attributes, the four states in life, the nature of the body and the self abiding in it, these are also dealt with.

(62. 14)

There are four kinds of states, namely waking, dream, sleep and the *turīya* (fourth). That in which there are fourteen instruments consisting of the senses of cognition and of action and of the four-fold internal organ, is the waking state. That which is associated only with the four-fold internal organ is the dream state. The state of sleep has the mind as the only instrument. The *turīya* is what is associated merely with the individual self.

ŚUKARAHASYA-UPANIṢAD

YAJUR-VEDA—TAITTIRĪYA

Here at the request of Vyāsa, Śiva imparts to Śuka, the son of Vyāsa, the teaching of the highest reality as contained in the Mahāvākya "That thou art".

(35. 21)

I salute that beneficent Teacher, who is the embodiment of eternal bliss, the giver of supreme happiness, the aloof, the embodiment of knowledge, transcending all, comparable to the sky, denoted by expressions like "That thou art", the one, eternal, free from impurity, immovable, the beholder of all cognitions, rising above forms, free from the triad of Guṇas.

(35. 22)

Now there are four great sentences. They are : Intelligence is Brahman. I am Brahman. That thou art. That self is Brahman.

SARVASĀRA-UPANIṢAD

YAJUR-VEDA—TAITTIRĪYA

Here there is a description of bondage and release, knowledge and ignorance, the four states of life, the five sheaths, the individual and his adjuncts, the self abiding in the body, the immutable self which is immanent, and such matters.

(33. 15)

What is called Māyā is beginningless, but having an end, common to right knowledge and erroneous knowledge, not real, not unreal, not real and unreal, in itself bigger than all, free from modifications, what is being thought of; though unreal and non-existent in three-fold time, it appears real to the ordinary people.

SĀVITRĪ-UPANIṢAD

SĀMA-VEDA

Here there is a description of the relation of the sun-god and the Gāyatrī. There is also a description of the mantras, Balā and Atibalā.

(75. 14)

Holding nectar at the end of their hands, able to give new life to all, extremely competent to remove sins, having the modification of the nature of Praṇava in the lustre of the essence of the Vedas, with bodies of the form of the sun, may I ever enjoy these two, the Balā and the Atibalā.

SUBĀLA-UPANIṢAD

YAJUR-VEDA—VĀJASANEYĪ

Here there is a description of the creation of the world and the various beings in the world. There is also the description of release and the path thereto.

(30. vi, 3-4)

The sons of Aditi, the Rudras, the Maruts, the Vasus, the twin Aśvins, the Ṛks, the Yajus, the Sāmans, the Mantra-Fire produced from the oblation of ghee, the divine, the god, such is the one Nārāyaṇa. Nārāyaṇa is father, mother, abode, refuge, friend and goal.

SŪRYA-UPANIṢAD

ATHARVA-VEDA

Here the sun-god is described as the supreme reality.

(71. 6)

Salutation to Mitra the shining. Protect me from death. Salutation to the resplendent, to the cause of all.

May the sun in the east, may the sun in the west, may the sun in the north, may the sun in the south, may the sun procure us everything. May the sun endow us with long life.

SKANDA-UPANIṢAD

YAJUR-VEDA—TAITTIRĪYA

Here Śiva and Viṣṇu are spoken of as absolutely identical.

(51..9)

Just as Viṣṇu is of the form of Śiva, so Śiva is of the nature of Viṣṇu. Let me have that fortune in life whereby I do not perceive any difference, whereby there will be no difference, no distinctions between Śiva and Keśava.

14

YOGA-UPANIṢADS

The twenty Upaniṣads, selections from which are given in this section, deal with the subject of yoga as an auxiliary path to knowledge. Eight stages—sometimes six—are distinguished in yoga. The first two, yama and niyama, afford preliminary moral training; they consist in shunning vices and acquiring cardinal virtues. The next three, āsana, prāṇāyāma and pratyāhāra, are intended for controlling the mind indirectly through rigorous physical discipline, symmetry and steadiness of body, regulation and stoppage of breath, and withdrawal of the senses from their objects. And the last three, dhāraṇā, dhyāna and samādhi are different stages in concentration; and they help directly in controlling the mind. The principal aim of yoga is to hold in check the unruly steeds of the senses, to still the stormy seas of the mind. When the mind is stilled, the veil is lifted, and the Real is attained with ease.

Since the topic is the same, there is much of repetition in these Upaniṣads. The different kinds of yoga are distinguished; the various yogic postures are described; the method of rousing the sleeping kuṇḍalinī to make it rush forth to the cerebral region is explained; and in some places the Vedāntic significance of the eight stages of yoga is given.

ADVAYATĀRAKA-UPANIṢAD

YAJUR-VEDA—VĀJASANEYĪ

It expounds the Rāja-yoga-as a means to Brahman-intuition. The yoga is called Tāraka because it enables one to ford the river of empirical existence.

(53. 2)

Contemplating always thus "I am of the nature of consciousness," with his eyes well closed, or with his eyes slightly open, seeing through the inner vision above the middle of the eyebrows, the supreme Brahman of the nature of the immutable effulgence of existence, consciousness and bliss, he (the ascetic) becomes of the form thereof.

AMṚTANĀDA-UPANIṢAD

YAJUR-VEDA—TAITTIRĪYA

It teaches that, while those who are pure in heart reach the goal even through the study, etc., of Scripture, those that are of impure heart stand in need of continued meditation on the Supreme and the practice of yoga with the six auxiliaries.

(21. 1)

Having studied the Scriptures, meditated again and again (on their import) and known the supreme Brahman, let the wise one give them up, as (he would) a firebrand.

AMṚTABINDU-UPANIṢAD

YAJUR-VEDA—TAITTIRĪYA

It points out that the mind of man is the cause of his bondage as well as release, and shows how Brahman is attainable through knowledge alone.

(20. 1-2)

The mind is said to be of two kinds, the pure and the impure; the impure (mind) is associated with desire, and the pure is devoid of desire.

The mind alone is the cause of the bondage and release of men; as attached to objects it leads to bondage, and as free from objects it leads to release.

KṢURIKA-UPANIṢAD

YAJUR-VEDA—TAITTIRĪYA

It deals with yoga as the instrument for removing the obstruction to Brahman-knowledge.

(31. 1)

I shall will relate the Kṣurikā (knife) of concentration for the sake of achieving yoga, attaining which there will be no rebirth for one who has accomplished yoga.

(31. 21)

He who has conquered his mind through penance (*i.e.*, *yoga*) remains in a silent place, unattached and desireless, and becomes gradually an adept in the yoga with its auxiliaries.

TEJOBINDU-UPANIṢAD

YAJUR-VEDA—TAITTIRĪYA

It deals with the realisation of ultimate release of the nature of impartite bliss and pure consciousness. The nature of the impartite bliss is also explained in this Upaniṣad by Śiva to his son Kumāra.

(37. i, 43)

Those, indeed, who live giving up this purifying, supreme psychosis (mental functioning) of the form of Brahman, live in vain; those men are the equals of brutes.

(37. i, 44)

Those, however, who know the psychosis and having known, increase it, are verily good men and fortunate. They are to be worshipped in the three worlds.

(37. i, 45)

Those, whose psychosis is even, increased and again matured—they verily attain the nature of Brahman, the real, not others who dispute about words.

(37. vi, 73, 75, 76)

If there be anything other than me, it is illusory even as water in the mirage. If the city of the Gandharvas were real, then the world ever exists. If in the sky blueness were real, then the world becomes real. If the shell-silver were a real ornament, then let the world be real.

TRIŚIKHIBRĀHMAṆA-UPANIṢAD

YAJUR-VEDA—VĀJASANEYĪ

In this we are told that a Brāhmin with three tufts went to the solar world and learnt the knowledge of Brahman, the order of creation, and the path of Yoga. We find here also a Vedāntic interpretation of the eight auxiliaries of classical yoga.

(44. i, 2)

He (the Lord) said: Know all this to be Śiva alone. But the eternal, pure, flawless, omnipresent non-dual bliss, Śiva, the one, having created all this by his own splendour, becomes one (therewith) like a burning mass of iron and shines as (also) different.

(44. i, 3)

From Brahman (came) the Unmanifest; from the Unmanifest, the Great (Mahat): from the Great, egoity; from egoity, the five subtle elements; from the five subtle elements, the five great elements; from the five great elements, the entire world.

(44. ii, 17)

Reaching hundreds of various wombs impelled by residual impressions, he (the jīva) lies; and strays away from release like the fish which wanders between the two banks (of a river).

DARŚANA-UPANIṢAD

SĀMA-VEDA

In this, Dattātreya imparts to the sage Sāṅkṛti the knowledge of the yoga with eight auxiliaries which leads to release in life. True worship is also defined.

(19. iv, 59)

The yogins see Śiva in the self, not in the images. The images have been created for the sake of contemplation by the ignorant.

(19. iv, 62)

Having known directly the bodiless among bodies, the great omnipresent Lord, the immutable bliss, the hero does not grieve.

DHYĀNABINDU-UPANIṢAD

YAJUR-VEDA—TAITTIRĪYA

It expounds the nature of Brahman and the import of the Praṇava; it teaches the Hamsa-vidyā and the yoga with six auxiliaries as the means to release.

(39. 1)

If there be sin, mountain-like and extending over several leagues, it is destroyed by the yoga of meditation. Never is there any other means of destruction.

(39. 61-62)

(The breath) goes out with the sound 'ha', and enters again with sound 'sa'. This mantra, *viz.*, 'hamsa', 'hamsa', the jīva mutters always.

(39. 63)

The Gāyatrī by name Ajapā (not consciously muttered) is always the giver of release to yogins.

NĀDABINDU-UPANIṢAD

ṚG-VEDA

It deals with the attainment of release through the destruction of the three kinds of Karma by those who are endowed with Nāda as the means.

(38. 27-28)

When the piece of rope is known, the form of snake does not remain. Likewise, when the substrate is known and when the universe (consequently) attains nullity, since the body too is of the universe, how can Prārabdha (*i.e.*, that part of one's past karma which has begun to take effect) remain ?

(38. 42)

Just as the bee which drinks the honey does not desire the scent, the mind which is ever absorbed in the Nāda (sound Om) does not desire the objects.

PĀŚUPATABRAHMA-UPANIṢAD

ATHARVA-VEDA

It deals with the nature of Hamsa and of Hiraṇyagarbha. Brahmā teaches this Upaniṣad to his son Vaiśravaṇa.

(77. i, 13)

Hamsa is of the nature of the supreme Self. Hamsa moves in and out.

(77. i, 19)

The sacred thread is the Praṇava. One who is engaged in the observance of Brahma-Yajña is a Brāhmaṇa. The gods move in the path of Brahman. The sacrifices are observances indicative of Hamsa. As between the Hamsa and the Praṇava there is no difference.

BRAHMAVIDYĀ-UPANIṢAD

YAJUR-VEDA—TAITTIRĪYA

In this also there is taught the knowledge of Hamsa and Praṇava as leading to Brahman-intuition. Incidentally we are told that teachers are of three kinds.

(40. 51-52)

The teacher in this world is said to be of three kinds thus: the one who commands, the one who imparts knowledge, and the supreme one who gives release. The one who commands shows the way; the one who imparts knowledge teaches the (supreme) place; and the one who gives release (reveals) the supreme truth, knowing which one attains immortality.

MAṆḌALABRĀHMAṆA-UPANIṢAD

YAJUR-VEDA—VĀJASANEYĪ

In this we are told that Yājñavalkya went to the solar world and learnt from the person in the solar orb the truth of the self and the subtle yoga with the eight auxiliaries.

(49. v, 1-3)

The mind as associated with objects leads to bondage, and as dissociated from objects to release. Hence all this world is the sphere of the mind. The same mind, when it is supportless and is ripe through the super-conscious state (in Nirvikalpaka samādhi) becomes fit for dissolution. That dissolution one should well practise in me, the full. I alone am the cause of the dissolution of the mind.

MAHĀVĀKYA-UPANIṢAD

ATHARVA-VEDA

In this, the Creator Brahmā teaches the great secret knowledge of the self.

(12. 8-9)

The one of the colour of the sun beyond darkness, recognising whom the wise man salutes and remains after pondering over all the forms and names and determining (that they are illusory); whose significance Brahmā explained in the beginning, and also Sakra (the king of the gods) whose fame aṣ a great knower had reached the four quarters; he who knows him thus becomes immortal here. There is no other way to the path (of release).

YOGAKUṆḌALĪ-UPANIṢAD

YAJUR-VEDA—TAITTIRĪYA

It explains the Haṭha Yoga and Lambikā Yoga.

(86. i, 82-83)

The auspicious power called Kuṇḍalinī, resembling the fibre of the lotus-stalk, having bitten the knot-like Mūlādhāra with the top of its hood, as if it were a lotus-root, and having grasped firmly the tail with its mouth, reaches the Brahmarandhra.

YOGACŪḌĀMAṆI-UPANIṢAD

SĀMA-VEDA

It deals with the six auxiliaries of yoga.

(46. 2)

Posture, complete control of breath, withdrawal (of the senses), contemplation, continued meditation, and absorption—these are the six auxiliaries of Yoga.

(46. 71)

Assuming the lotus-pose aright, holding the trunk and head erect in a line, and looking at the tip of the nose, let one mutter in solitude the imperishable Oṁkāra.

YOGATATTVA-UPANIṢAD

YAJUR-VEDA—TAITTIRĪYA

It sets forth the four kinds of yoga : Mantra, Laya, Haṭha and Rāja.

(41. 19)

O Brahmā, yoga, indeed, is of many kinds due to usage : Mantra-yoga, Laya, Haṭha and Rāja-yoga.

(41. 129-130)

When the actions (yogic practices) have been accomplished by yogins through Rāja-yoga, then arises surely for the yogins detachment through discrimination.

YOGAŚIKHĀ-UPANIṢAD

YAJUR-VEDA—TAITTIRĪYA

It deals with the path of knowledge in all its aspects. Yoga and knowledge are said to be complementary to each other. The teaching is given by Śaṅkara, the supreme Lord, to Hiraṇyagarbha.

(63. i, 13-14)

How can knowledge devoid of yoga become the giver of release here, O Sir? Yoga, too, which is devoid of knowledge is not capable of effecting release. Therefore, knowledge and yoga let the one who longs for release practise.

VARĀHA-UPANIṢAD

YAJUR-VEDA—TAITTIRĪYA

It deals with the ninety-six tattvas and gives an exposition of the path of knowledge, the nature of Brahman, and the import of Praṇava. The teaching is given to the sage Ribhu by the Lord (Viṣṇu) in the form of a Boar. Then Ribhu gives a description of release in life and the seven stages of knowledge to Nidāgha.

(98. ii, 3-4)

Discrimination between the eternal and the non-eternal, non-attachment (to the enjoyment of fruits) here and in a hereafter, possession of the six qualities, tranquillity, etc., longing for release—one should cultivate these.

(98. ii, 41)

If one knows "Brahman exists", that is only mediate knowledge. If one knows "I am Brahman", that is called immediate experience.

ŚĀṆḌILYA-UPANIṢAD

ATHARVA-VEDA

In this, Atharvan relates to Śāṇḍilya the eight

auxiliaries of yoga and the attainment of Brahman thereby.

(58. 1, 24)

Two ways there are of destroying the mind—yoga and knowledge, O Sage ! Yoga is obstructing the psychosis (mental functions), and knowledge is clear insight.

(58. 1, 25)

When the (mental functioning) is obstructed, the mind becomes quiescent soon. And when the movement of mind is stopped, transmigration gets resolved.

HAMSA-UPANIṢAD

YAJUR-VEDA—VĀJASANEYĪ

In this, Gautama learns from Sanatkumāra the knowledge of Brahman and the means thereto, viz., Hamsa-vidyā.

(25. 4)

We shall now explain clearly the mode of determining Hamsa and Paramahamsa for the sake of the religious student who is self-controlled, who is devoted to his master, and who meditates always thus : 'Hamsa, Hamsa'.

(25. 5)

Pervading all bodies it (the Hamsa) exists, as fire in the fuel and as oil in the sesamum seeds. Having known that, one does not reach death.

15

SAMNYĀSA-UPANIṢADS

There are seventeen Upaniṣads in which Samnyāsa as an antecedent step for the realisation of Brahman forms the main subject-matter. Samnyāsa is only an accessory and not an end in itself. The various types of persons who have renounced the world, their duties, the necessary prerequisites for Samnyāsa the evil effect of premature samnyāsa and fraudulent renunciation are all clearly explained in these Upaniṣads. Samnyāsa should come in the natural course of the evolution of the soul and should not be imposed by force from outside. Suppression or repression of man's worldly needs is condemned as much as the glories of a true saint are extolled.

AVADHŪTA-UPANIṢAD

YAJUR-VEDA—TAITTIRĪYA

Here the nature of an Avadhūta is described. He transcends dualisms in the world like virtue and vice and has cast away every belonging.

(71. 9)

Just as the sun absorbs water from everywhere, and just as fire too eats everything, in the same way the Yogin enjoys all objects and (yet), being pure, is not tainted by merits and sins.

ĀRUṆI-UPANIṢAD

SĀMA-VEDA

Here the nature of one who is ready to renounce, the process of renouncing, and the rules of conduct for those who have renounced and such other matters are dealt with.

(16. 4)

By the wandering mendicants who are Paramahamsas and who are dedicated to Brahman (life should be led) by sitting and sleeping on the ground. Their vessels shall be of earth, of gourd, or of wood. During rainy season for eight months, a samnyāsin shall live in solitude with a steady conduct. (Or he shall so live) only for two months.

KAṬHARUDRA-UPANIṢAD

YAJUR-VEDA—TAITTIRĪYA

Here renunciation as a step towards the knowledge of Brahman is described. Dedication to the knowledge of Brahman and its fruits are also dealt with.

(83. 4)

After renouncing, one shall not again return to the care of the household fire. Saying "weal to all living beings", he shall live without a habitation, thinking of the self, and without (thinking of) anything else. Eating food got by alms, he need not give anything.

KUṆḌIKĀ-UPANIṢAD

SĀMA-VEDA

The stages preceding renunciation, the eligibility for renunciation, namely, loss of the wife, purpose of renunciation being getting release from life, prohibition of return to the life of a householder and the conduct of one who has renounced are described here.

(74. 15-16)

He shall sleep on the sands on river banks or outside of temples. He shall not fatigue his body too much either through enjoyment or through mortification.

Bathing, drinking, similarly cleaning, these he shall perform with clean water. He shall not feel elated by flattery. Being abused he shall not curse others.

JĀBĀLA-UPANIṢAD

YAJUR-VEDA—VĀJASANEYĪ

Renunciation of all rites, eligibility for renunciation, renunciation of a householder and of one who has not assumed the role of a householder, the nature of a Paramahamsa and such matters are dealt with here.

(13. iv, 1)

After finishing the life of religious student, one shall enter the life of a householder. After completing the life of a householder, he shall become a forest-dweller (ascetic). After retiring to the forest, he shall renounce. Or if it be otherwise, he can renounce even as a religious student or as a householder or as an ascetic. Or again, as a religious student or not as a religious student, either as a bachelor or not as a bachelor, either after finishing the tending of the household fire or without any fire, if on any day he feels non-attachment to the world, on that very day he can renounce.

TURĪYATĪTĀVADHŪTA-UPANIṢAD

YAJUR–VEDA—VĀJASANEYĪ

The nature of one who has discarded all possessions and who has transcended the four stages of life is described in this short text.

(64. 1)

He who treads the path of an Avadhūta is very rare in this world, not to be had in plenty. If there is one, he alone is the ever pure. He alone is the embodiment of non-attachment to the world. He alone is of the form of knowledge. He alone is the Person of the form of the Vedas. He, the Paramahamsa, transcends the fourfold stages of life, dedicates himself to steady non-dualism as an Avadhūta and casts off his body, being himself of the nature of the syllable Om.

NĀRADAPARIVRĀJAKA-UPANIṢAD

ATHARVA-VEDA

The rules of conduct for the four stages of life, the different types of persons who have renounced, the eligibility for renunciation, evil effects of renouncing prematurely, nature of Brahman for whose knowledge renunciatian is an antecedent step and various other matters are described in this Upaniṣad which is a very long one.

(43. iii, 12-13)

When non-attachment to all activities arises in the mind, then they desire renunciation. Through a contrary procedure one becomes fallen. A wise man shall renounce when he becomes non-attached. But one who is attached shall abide in his home. He who is full of attachment enters hell as the lowest of the twice-born if he renounces.

NIRVĀṆA-UPANIṢAD

ṚG-VEDA

In this short and very abstruse and obscure text the special features of a real Samnyāsin who has reached the Avadhūta stage are described.

(47. 38-40)

Seeing the real bliss-form through Yoga : eating the bliss-alms : even in the burial ground, life is in the garden of bliss.

PARABRAHMA-UPANIṢAD

YAJUR-VEDA—VĀJASANEYĪ

The superiority of Brahman-knowledge, the nature of Brahman, and the rules of conduct for one who has renounced are described here.

(78. 14)

They who are eligible only for active life, either worldly or scriptural, live (as Samnyāsins) to fill their stomach merely as pseudo-Brāhmaṇas.

PARAMAHAMSAPARIVRĀJAKA-UPANIṢAD

ATHARVA-VEDA

The eligibility for renunciation and the nature of Brahman as the syllable Om, knowledge, steadfastness and other virtues which are the invisible marks of a Brāhmaṇa superior to the visible tuft and the sacred thread : these are dealt with here.

(66. 5)

To him who has the knowledge of the self without a second, that itself is his sacred thread. To him steadfastness in the self is itself the tuft. He is the performer of all rites. He is the Brāhmaṇa. He is superior to all. He himself am I (Viṣṇu).

PARAMAHAMSA-UPANIṢAD

YAJUR-VEDA—VĀJASANEYĪ

The path of the Paramahamsa and the nature of such a one and fraudulence of persons posing as Samnyāsins are dealt with here.

(19. 3)

He by whom is carried a wooden stick, who eats anything, who is devoid of knowledge, who is devoid of virtues like desire to renounce, knowledge, non-attachment and tranquillity, who lives simply for alms, he is a sinner who destroys the conduct of a Saint. He goes to terrible hells known as Mahāraurava.

BRAHMA-UPANIṢAD

YAJUR-VEDA—TAITTIRĪYA

The real nature of Brahman, external marks like tuft which are only for those who are leading the worldly life, and renunciation as a means of attaining Brahman are described here.

(11. 12-13)

He for whom, as for fire there is no other tuft, for whom the tuft is of the form of knowledge, he, the knowing one, is said to be endowed with a (real) tuft, not others who wear a tuft of hair. But those Brāhmaṇas and others who are eligible for Vedic rituals, by them is this thread to be worn. Indeed, that is prescribed verily as a part of the rites.

BHIKṢUKA-UPANIṢAD

YAJUR–VEDA—VĀJASANEYĪ

The four kinds of wandering mendicants are described in this very short text. Hamsa and Paramahamsa are better known and their description is not given in this selection.

(60. 1-2)

Among mendicants who seek after release, there are four orders, namely, Kuṭīcaka, Bahūdaka, Hamsa and Paramahamsa. They are called Kuṭīcakas who, living on eight handfuls of food, seek after release along the Path of Yoga. Then they are called Bahūdakas who, having a three-spiked stick, a vessel, a tuft, sacred thread and yellow robes and managing their lives on charity in the abodes of Brāhmaṇa-sages avoiding wine and meat, seek after release along the Path of Yoga.

MAITREYĪ-UPANIṢAD

YAJUR–VEDA—VĀJASANEYĪ

Purification of mind and other internal organs, renunciation of self-ness and worldly rites, the nature of real renunciation, the value of realisation and such things are dealt with here.

(21. ii, 23)

They without realisation are the deluded who enjoy Brahman in vain, like enjoying the taste of fruits on the end of branches reflected in water.

(21. ii, 25)

Those who are great in riches, those who are great in age, and similarly those who are great in erudition, all these are mere servants of those who are great in wisdom, or even the servants of their pupils.

YĀJÑAVALKYA-UPANIṢAD

YAJUR–VEDA–VĀJASANEYĪ

The rites associated with renunciation, those who are eligible for renunciation, the duties of those who are not so eligible, the nature of a Paramahamsa, the identity of a wandering mendicant with the supreme Lord, renunciation of worldly enjoyments and the nature of a true saint are described here.

(17. 11)

Misguided, with their minds turned outward, mean and fond of quarrel, even Samnyāsins of this nature are seen whose minds are spoiled by the (wrong) Vedic teachings.

(17. 12)

If one is established in that greatness, in that self-overlordship without a second, beyond the scope of names and others, then he who knows the self, whom shall he bow to? He has at that time no need of deeds.

ŚĀṬHYĀYANĪYA-UPANIṢAD

YAJUR-VEDA—VĀJASANEYĪ

Mind as the cause of bondage and release, the four kinds of Samnyāsins and their duties, the life of a wandering mendicant, the danger of falling off after trying to ascend and such matters are dealt with here.

(99. 20)

With a bowl, with a stick, looking ahead only one yard, shaven (and yet) with (knowledge as) tuft, with (steadfastness in knowledge as) sacred thread, with (himself alone as,) family, accepting alms from men, either begging, or without begging, just for keeping on life (such is the true saint).

SAMNYĀSA-UPANIṢAD

SĀMA-VEDA

Those who are eligible and those who are not eligible for renunciation, the different classes of those who have renounced, the duties of those who have renounced and such matters are described in this fairly long Upaniṣad.

(65. ii, 18)

One who renounces through non-attachment, one who renounces through knowledge, one who renounces through non-attachment and knowledge and one who merely renounces the rituals : those who renounce are thus four-fold.

16

VAIṢṆAVA-UPANIṢADS

There are fourteen minor Upaniṣads dealing with Viṣṇu and His manifold forms. Viṣṇu is described as identical with the highest reality, from whom emanate all beings, including all the gods, who supports the entire universe and into whom the universe resolves at the end. Various mantras relating to the worship of the different forms of Viṣṇu, the prescription for their proper recitation and their efficacy, the eligibility for their recitation and such matters are dealt with. Narasimha, Śrī-Rāma, Hayagrīva and Dattātreya are some of the forms of Viṣṇu. Devotion to Viṣṇu and his worship according to the prescribed method are the only unfailing means for the attainment of the ultimate goal of man.

Many of the Upaniṣads are very long; and three of them are divided into two main sections as Pūrva (former) *and Uttara (latter.)*

AVYAKTA-UPANIṢAD

SĀMA-VEDA

The creator was able to see Viṣṇu in the form of Man-Lion through the power of an Anuṣṭup verse and with his grace created the entire world out of the thirty syllables of the verse. This is described here.

(68. ii, 1)

Then he saw the Ṛk in the Anuṣṭup metre, which is the supreme knowledge, of which other mantras are only limbs, in which Brahman is well established and all the gods are well established. He who does not know that (Ṛk in the Anuṣṭup metre), what will he do with the other Vedas ?

KALISANTARAṆA-UPANIṢAD

YAJUR-VEDA—TAITTRĪYA

Uttering the name Nārāyaṇa is here described as capable of removing all sins.

(103. 1)

At the end of the Dvāpara Yuga, Nārada went to Brahmā and asked : Venerable Sir, when I am wandering about in the world, how am I to get over Kali ? Then Brahmā said : I have been asked a good question. Listen to that mystery which is the secret of all scriptures whereby you can get over the transmigration in Kali. By the mere utterance of the name of Lord Nārāyaṇa, the first Person, one can get rid of Kali.

KṚṢṆA-UPANIṢAD

ATHARVA-VEDA

Śrī Rāma promises the sages of the forest to come down again as Kṛṣṇa, full incarnation of Viṣṇu, for their satisfaction and joy.

(96. 1)

The sages living in the forest became wonderstruck when they saw Rāmacandra of ravishing beauty, who is the Great Viṣṇu himself, who can be defined only as Reality, Knowledge and Bliss. They said to him : May we embrace you ? He replied : In the next cycle, when I come down as Kṛṣṇa, you become the milkmaids and then you embrace me.

GARUḌA-UPANIṢAD

ATHARVA-VEDA

The mantra for propitiating Garuḍa, the vehicle of Viṣṇu, and the prescribed method of its recitation are decribed here.

(102. 10)

Om ! salutation to the great and venerable Garuḍa, the vehicle of Viṣṇu, revered by all the three worlds, with claws made of steel and beak also made of steel, with his body adorned with wings made of steel. Come, come, great Garuḍa. Cut off, cut off the poison. Revive, revive (me).

GOPĀLATĀPINA-UPANIṢAD

ATHARVA-VEDA

This Upaniṣad contains two sections called the former (pūrva) and the latter (uttara). The first two selections are from the first section, and the third is from the second section. Gopāla is identical with the Supreme. Devotion to Him is the means for release. The world was created out of a mantra dedicated to him. In the second section there is a glorification of Kṛṣṇa's City, Mathurā.

(15 i, 14)

Devotion is dedication to him. That (dedication) is attaching the mind to Him, free from all desires for the adjuncts in this or in the next world. And this itself is freedom from actions.

(15. i, 15)

Wise men perform sacrifices to him Kṛṣṇa, in various ways. They worship Him who is Govinda, in various ways. The lord of milkmaids supports the worlds. Relying on Svāhā, he impels the world, being endowed with energy.

(15. 28)

(The gods live) having gone to the beautiful Mathurā, which is worshipped by Brahmā, Rudra and others, which is protected by the conch, by the disc, by the club, by the bow and by the mace and other things, where abides this Kṛṣṇa in the company of women and of Śakti, the Lord accompanied by Balarāma, Aniruddha, Pradyumna and Rukmiṇī.

TĀRASĀRA-UPANIṢAD

YAJUR–VEDA—VĀJASANEYĪ

In this Upaniṣad, some mantras relating to Viṣṇu as Śrī Rāma are given. Śrī Rāma is identified with the various persons associated with him, like Jambavān, Hanumān and Lakṣmaṇa.

(12. i, 5)

The mantra 'Om Namo Nārāyaṇāya' (Om salutation to Nārāyaṇa) one must worship as of the form of knowledge, which takes one across (transmigration). The one syllabic part 'Om' is of the form of the self. The two syllabic part 'Namaḥ' (salutation) is of the form of the world. The five syllabic part 'Nārāyaṇāya' (to Nārāyaṇa) is of the form of the supreme Brahman.

(In Om na-mo-nā-rā-ya-ṇā-ya) Om is Brahmā. The sound na is Viṣṇu. The sound ma is Rudra. The sound na is God. The sound ra is the Lord of the Egg. The sound ya is the person. The sound na is the Lord. The sound ya is the supreme self.

TRIPĀDVIBHŪTI-MAHĀNĀRĀYAṆA-UPANIṢAD

ATHARVA–VEDA

This is a very long Upaniṣad in which Nārāyaṇa is identified with the supreme reality.

The apparent contradiction of the formless Absolute being identical with Nārāyaṇa having a form is explained. Knowledge of Nārāyaṇa and devotion arising therefrom lead to final release.

(92. v, 8)

When one gets the kind glances of a good teacher, then there arises in him a strong desire to listen to and to contemplate the stories about the Lord. Thence arises the destruction of the knots of evil impression abiding in the heart without a beginning. From that arises the appearance of the supreme soul in the lotus petals of the heart. Thence comes about devotion to Viṣṇu of a very steadfast nature.

DATTĀTREYA-UPANIṢAD

YAJUR-VEDA—VĀJASANEYĪ

In this there are described various mantras pertaining to Viṣṇu as Dattātreya.

(101. i, 1)

In the abode of Truth, Brahmā asked Nārāyaṇa of wide domain : What is it that takes us across ? O Lord, tell me that. Being thus addressed, he replied : Worship my abode of purity, of the nature of Truth, Bliss and Knowledge. They who always say this : I am given, they do not get entangled in transmigration. Brahmā being thus instructed by

Nārāyaṇa, meditated on Viṣṇu, Nārāyaṇa, Dattātreya, who assumes the cosmic form and said : It is the reality.

NĀRĀYAṆA-UPANIṢAD

YAJUR-VEDA—TAITTIRĪYA

In this Upaniṣad, Nārāyaṇa is described as the source from which everything and every god originate and as of the nature of all. There is the the Nārāyaṇa mantra by reciting which one attains the highest goal.

(18. iv)

One who meditates on the mantra 'Om, salutation to Nārāyaṇa' will reach Vaikuṇṭha as his abode. That is the lotus, the knowledge-mass. Therefore, it is of the brightness of lightning.

The son of Devakī is of the nature of Brahman. The destroyer of Madhu is of the nature of Brahman. (I worship) Nārāyaṇa who abides in all beings, who is the person that is the cause, who has no cause, who is Brahman. Om !

NṚSIMHATĀPINĪ-UPANIṢAD

ATHARVA-VEDA

This is divided into two parts. A selection is given from each part. This is a very long one, in which the Nṛsimha-mantra is described as the cause of the world. Detailed prescriptions are given regarding its recitation and its efficacy.

(27. ii, 1)

The gods were afraid of death, of sins and of transmigration. They went to Prajāpati. To them he gave this Nṛsimha mantra, the king of mantras, in the Anuṣṭup metre. Indeed, thereby they conquered death. They crossed the sins. They also crossed transmigration. Therefore, he who is afraid of death, of sins and of transmigration, shall accept this king of mantras in the Anuṣṭup metre.

(27. iii, 10)

Then worshipping these (parts of the syllable Om) in four ways with the nectar of bliss, similarly worshipping the three undivided ones of the nature of separate marks, divided only as Brahmā, only as Viṣṇu and only as Rudra, bringing together the marks with objects of worship in four ways, pervading the three bodies with light, kindling the self that abides in it, controlling the power, that light of the nature of the sentience of the self, bringing about identification with the constituents of the world, reducing the very gross into the very subtle, and the very subtle into the great cause, and contemplating it as being qualified by the knower and knowledge which are woven through with the elements of the Om : thus one should accept the Om.

RĀMATĀPINĪ-UPANIṢAD

ATHARVA-VEDA

Here there is a description of the various mantras about Śrī Rāma and their efficacy in securing the highest ends for man. This Upaniṣad too is in two parts and selections are given from both.

(55. iii, 1)

Sītā and Rāma are of that nature (of the mantra) and are to be worshipped. The twice seven worlds are created from them. They are supported in them; to them they are sent (in the end). Therefore Rāma becoming a man gave prosperity (to the world) with his Māyā.

Let there be salutation to him who is the self, the Life of the universe. Salutation. One should declare their identity on account of their former constituents (of reality, bliss and knowledge).

(55. iii, 15-16)

They who learn the mantra of six syllables either from you or from Brahmā shall have everything secured through the mantra when alive, and when released (from life) they will come to me. If at the time of death of any one whatsoever, this mantra of mine shall be recited in the right ear, he shall, O Śiva, be released.

(55. v, 6)

The mantra of Sri Rama is more efficacious in securing the desired end than the mantras of Gaṇapati, the mantras of Śakti and the mantras of Sūrya. Even among the Mantras of Viṣṇu, it is the most efficacious in securing fruits.

RĀMARAHASYA-UPANIṢAD

ATHARVA–VEDA

Various Rāma-mantras are described here. There is a special glorification of the mantra with eight syllables. Detailed prescription for their recitation and their efficacy are given in this Upaniṣad.

(54. ii, 38)

Why should one trouble himself in vain with many mantras whose fruits are liable to destruction and which can be uttered only with great difficulty, which become powerless by merely being uttered with even the slightest defect and which only keep up the miseries of transmigration ? This mantra of eight syllables "Śrī Rāma is my refuge" (Śrī Rā-maḥ śa-ra-ṇam ma-ma), though only one, is capable of securing the fruits of all mantras and ever free from evils like longing.

VĀSUDEVA-UPANIṢAD

SĀMA-VEDA

In this Upaniṣad there is a glorification of Gopīcandana as the most favourite object of Viṣṇu.

(56. 2)

The Viṣṇucandana, that has its source in Vaikuṇṭha, that gives me pleasure, that is worn by my devotees like Brahmā, that is every day smeared on my body, and that, since it is washed away by the Gopīs (milk-maids), is called Gopīcandana, that is the smearing stuff for my body, that is holy, that abides within the Cakratīrtha, that is associated with Cakra, that has a yellow colour : this is the means for release.

HAYAGRĪVA-UPANIṢAD

ATHARVA-VEDA

Viṣṇu as Hayagrīva, having the head of a horse, the teacher of humanity, is described in the Upaniṣad.

(102. 3)

Salutation to you. O Hayagrīva, whose form transcends the entire universe, whose form is that of Bliss of the nature of knowledge, who is the king of wisdom, who is Viṣṇu.

(102. 4)

Salutation to Him who is of the form of Ṛk, Yajus and Sāman, who has performed the deed of restoring the Vedas, whose body is the syllable Om and the Sāman chant.

17

ŚAIVA-UPANIṢADS

Besides the Śvetāśvatara, selections from which have been given already, there are fourteen Upaniṣads which eulogise Rudra, identify him with the Supreme Brahman, and make him the source and support of all things. The rudiments of the Rudra-Śiva cult are traceable to the age of the Indus valley civilisation. In the Ṛg-veda, Rudra figures for the most part as the terrible God holding a thunderbolt in his arms and sending forth lightning shafts from the skies. The Svetāśvatara makes him out to be auspicious, unterrific, indicating no evil, the primal cause of all beings. The other Saiva Upaniṣads continue the same thought and identify Rudra with the absolute. He is the lord (pati) of souls (paśu). There is no real difference between God and soul. The difference is only apparent, brought about by avidyā. At the onset of knowledge, ignorance disappears, and the individual recognises his real self as Śiva. A good part of these Upaniṣads is taken up with a detailed description of the visible marks of a Śaiva, viz., the rosary of Rudrākṣa-beads and the sacred ash : the mode of wearing them and the mantras to be used are explained. These external marks are regarded as auxiliaries to Brahman-intuition. They are helpful in the path to Perfection.

AKṢAMĀLIKA-UPANIṢAD

ṚG-VEDA

In this Upaniṣad Prajāpati learns from Guha the details concerning rosaries : their kinds and constituents, the inner significance of the various parts, the mantras that are to be used while telling the beads, their fruit, etc.

(67. 3)

That which is the inner thread is Brahman. That which is on the right side (silver thread) is to be considered as belonging to Śiva. That which is on the left (copper thread) belongs to Viṣṇu. That which is the face is Sarasvatī. That which is the bottom is Gāyatrī. That which is the hole is knowledge. That which is the knot is Prakṛti.

ATHARVAŚIKHA-UPANIṢAD

ATHARVA-VEDA

In this Upaniṣad, Atharvan teaches the significance of Om and the meditation thereon; and Śiva is declared to be the supreme object of meditation.

(23. iii, 4)

All this is Brahma, Viṣṇu, Rudra and Indra. They create all sense organs along with the elements. (These elements, etc.,) are not the cause. The cause of (all) causes is the one who meditates. The object of meditation (too) is Śambhu, the giver of happiness, the lord of all, endowed with all auspicious powers. If a person concentrates for an instant (on Śiva) in the ether of his heart steadily, he attains greater fruit than can be attained by a hundred and seventy-four sacrifices; the entire path of Om (is also known by him). He who knows Omkāra thus attains the fruit of all the yogas of meditation and knowledge. Śiva, the one, is to be meditated on as the supreme Lord and giver of happiness, leaving all else.

ATHARVAŚIRA-UPANIṢAD

ATHARVA-VEDA

In this Upaniṣad Rudra declares himself to the gods to be all in all. The gods in turn pray to Rudra identifying him with the Supreme.

(22. 1)

The gods went to the heavenly world. Those gods asked Rudra : Who are you ?

(22. 2)

He said : I am one; existed at first, exist (now), and will exist (for all time) ; no other there is which is different from me.

KĀLĀGNIRUDRA-UPANIṢAD

YAJUR-VEDA—TAITTIRĪYA

In this Upaniṣad, Sanatkumāra learns from Kālāgni-Rudra the method to be followed in smearing ashes.

(28. 3)

The material is the burnt ash. Taking it (with the right hand and placing it on the left) with the Pañca-Brahma-mantras, Sadyojāta, etc., consecrating it (touching it with the right hand) with the (Pañcabhūta) mantras 'fire is the ash', 'air is the ash', 'ether is the ash', 'water is the ash', 'earth is the ash' taking it well (again) with the mantra 'mā nastoke tanaya', mixing it with water with the mantra 'mā no mahāntam', and (placing) it on the head, forehead, chest and shoulders with the mantra 'triyāyuṣam jamadagneḥ', let one make three lines with the 'triyāyuṣa' mantras, with the 'tryambaka' mantras and with the mantras that speak of the three Powers (Durgā, Lakṣmī and Sarasvatī). This observance to Śambhu is (regarded as) said in all the Vedas by those who are of the Vedic school. Therefore, let him who desires release observe this rite so as not to be born again.

KAIVALYA-UPANIṢAD

YAJUR-VEDA—TAITTIRĪYA

In this Upaniṣad, Śiva is identified with the

supreme Brahman, the source of all ; the non-difference between the jīva and the Lord is declared ; and the experience of non-difference is explained.

(12. 6-7)

Unthinkable, unmanifest, endless in form, Śiva, the peaceful immortal Brahmā-source, devoid of beginning, middle and end, the one all-pervading consciousness-bliss, formless and wonderful, the consort of Umā, the supreme God, the Lord with three eyes, blue throat, and peaceful—meditating on him the ascetic attains him, the source of beings, the witness of all, beyond darkness.

(12. 8-9)

He is Brahmā; he is Śiva; he is Indra; he is the immutable, the supreme self-ruler; he alone is Viṣṇu; he is Life; he is Time; he is Fire; he is the Moon. He alone is all, what has been and what will be; he is the eternal. Knowing him, one overcomes death. No. other path there is for release.

GAṆAPATI-UPANIṢAD

ATHARVA-VEDA

In this Upaniṣad meditation on Gaṇapati as the supreme is prescribed.

(89. 11 and 14)

The God with one tusk, four arms, having a noose (in one hand) and a goad (in the second), offering shelter (with the third) and giving boons (with the fourth), bearing the banner with the mouse-emblem, who manifested himself at the beginning of creation, and who is superior to prakṛti and puruṣa—he who meditates on him always thus is a yogin, the best of yogins.

JĀBĀLI-UPANIṢAD

SĀMA-VEDA

In this Upaniṣad the terms 'Paśupati; (God) and 'Paśu' (soul) are explained; smearing of ashes is declared to be the means to knowledge; and the method of smearing is also set forth.

(107. 11)

The Lord of souls (Paśupati) as endowed with egoity is the transmigrating self. He alone is the soul (Paśu). The Lord of souls is God, the ruler of all, endowed with the five acts (creation, etc.,) and omniscient.

(107. 12)

The jīvas are said to be bound souls; being their Lord, God is Paśupati.

DAKṢIṆĀMŪRTI-UPANIṢAD

YAJUR-VEDA—TAITTIRĪYA

In this Upāniṣad, Śiva is identified with

Dakṣiṇāmūrti. Knowledge of this identity is said to be the supreme secret, the harbinger of longevity and of ultimate release.

(49. 13)

The Lord Dakṣiṇāmūrti, whose body is white on account of the sacred ash, who wears the crescent, whose lotus-like hands shine with the symbol of knowledge, rosary, the lyre and the book, who is beautiful with the yoga-band, who is seated expounding (knowledge), who is attended by groups of saints, who is pleased, who has the serpent (on his person) and is clad in hides—may he protect us always.

PAÑCABRAHMA-UPANIṢAD

YAJUR-VEDA—TAITTIRĪYA

In this Upaniṣad, Mahādeva, the supreme God, teaches the five forms of Brahman that arose at first: Sadyojāta, Aghora, Vāmadeva, Tatpuruṣa, and Īśāna. Īśāna is the highest form; but all the five are to be resolved in the supreme Brahman which is really without form.

(13. 19)

Know Īśāna as the supreme impeller, witness of the intellect, etherial in nature, unmanifest, and adorned with the sound Om.

(13. 22)

The supreme Brahman shines by its own light beyond the five Brahman-forms. In the beginning, at the end, and in the middle it shines by no other means.

BṚHAJJĀBĀLA-UPANIṢAD

ATHARVA–VEDA

In this Upaniṣad are set forth the greatness of the sacred ash, the significance of its various names, the mode of its production, the rite of bathing in ash, the way of smearing the ash on the different parts of the body, the mantras to be used in these rites, etc. There is also to be found the derivative meaning of the world 'Rudrākṣa'.

(26. i, 15)

Vibhūti, Bhasita, Bhasma, Kṣāra, Rakṣā : these are the five names, of the sacred ash. Of the five names, because it is the cause of supreme prosperity, it (the sacred ash) is called Bhūti. Because it eats up all sin, it is called Bhasma. Because it shines, it is called Bhasita. Because it wards off dangers, it is called Kṣāra. Because it protects one well from ghosts, departed spirits, devils, evil spirits, epilepsy and the fear of birth, it is called Rakṣā.

(26. vii, 16)

Because they emanated from the eyes of Rudra, they (the Rudrākṣa-beads) are called Rudrākṣas in the world. After destroying (the world), Sadāśiva closed his eye of destruction. The Rudrākṣas emanated therefrom.

BHASMAJĀBĀLA-UPANIṢAD

ATHARVA–VEDA

In this Upaniṣad the method of wearing the ash-marks is explained; the various rites connected therewith are described; the worship of Śiva according to rule is prescribed; and life in Benares is enjoined on those who are incapable of higher worship.

(87. i, 8)

For Brāhmaṇas, this alone is the religious duty; this alone is religious duty. Without wearing the ash-marks thus, let one not take water, food or any other thing. Without wearing the ash-marks due to carelessness, let one not mutter the Gāyatrī; let one not offer oblation in fire, let one not offer libation to the gods, to the seers and to the manes. This alone is the old religious duty which destroys all sin and causes release.

RUDRAHṚDAYA-UPANIṢAD

YAJUR-VEDA—TAITTIRĪYA

In this Upaniṣad, Rudra is declared to be of the nature of all; Śiva, Viṣṇu, Brahmā, and Umā are regarded as different manifestations of the same Spirit; the difference between the higher knowledge and lower knowledge is explained; the difference between the jīva and the Lord is charac-

terised as apparent; and the knowledge of non-difference is said to remove sorrow and delusion.

(85. 5-6)

Those who salute Govinda do salute Śaṅkara. Those who worship Hari do worship the one with the bull-banner.

Those who hate Virūpākṣa hate Janārdana (also). Those who do not know Rudra do not know Keśava also.

RUDRĀKṢAJĀBĀLA-UPANIṢAD

SĀMA-VEDA

In this Upaniṣad, Bhusuṇḍa learns from Kālāgni-Rudra details regarding the Rudrabeads, their origin, eligibility to wear them, conditions of wearing them, etc.

(88. 2)

To him the Lord Kālāgni-Rudra said : For the sake of killing the demon of Tripura, I remained with open eyes. From them teardrops fell on earth. They became Rudrākṣas.

ŚARABHA-UPANIṢAD

ATHARVA-VEDA

In this Upaniṣad, the creator Brahmā proclaims Rudra to be the supreme God; it is also said that Rudra in the form of a Śarabha (a fabulous animal considered to be stronger than the lion) killed a Nṛsimha; the gods praise Rudra who has assumed this great form; and finally it is declared that there is no difference between Śiva and Viṣṇu.

(50. 3)

Brahmā said :

Only by those who have performed many meritorious deeds is attained this supreme Lord from whose limbs I was born as also Hari and Indra. Through delusion the king of the gods, Indra, and others do not know (this).

18

ŚĀKTA-UPANIṢADS

Śakti forms the theme of eight Minor Upaniṣads. In one of the hymns of the Ṛg-veda, Śakti is characterised as residing in heaven and supporting the earth. In the Kena-upaniṣad she appears as Umā Haimavatī revealing the knowledge of the Supreme to the gods. The worship of the Mother-Goddess is an answer to a vital need of the human heart.

Śakti is regarded as the spouse of Śiva. She is also identified with the other goddesses. Lakṣmī, Sarasvatī, and others. Śakti is the Power of God; and as power and the one who has power are non-different, Śiva and Śakti are inseparable. The creation of the universe is attributed to Śakti. Three forms of Power by which the world is ruled are recognised; Power as will (icchā), Power as knowledge (jñāna) and Power as action (kriyā). Ultimately, Śakti is identified with Māyā which creates an apparent fissure in Reality and veils the Truth.

The worship of Śakti is said to give to the devotee not only prosperity but also final release. The Śākta-upaniṣads contain descriptions of Cakras and Mudras that are used in rituals connected with Śakti. These rituals are elabora-

tely treated in the Tantras which, in later Hinduism, led to certain malpractices. The real object of the Tāntric discipline, however, is to sublimate the lower impulses and help the soul to reach its destiny.

TRIPURA-UPANIṢAD

ṚG–VEDA

In this Upaniṣad, the nature of Consciousness-Power is described; the different modes of meditation on Śakti are set forth : and it is said that the selfless worship of the Goddess leads to final release.

(82. 1)

The three cities (the causal, subtle and gross bodies) and the three roads (work, worship and wisdom) assumed by the empirical soul, and the letters beginning with 'a' which are well set here (in the Śrī-cakra)—supporting these (shines the Consciousness-Power), the supreme Greatness of the gods, ancient and unaging.

TRIPURĀTĀPINĪ-UPANIṢAD

ATHARVA–VEDA

In this Upaniṣad, the nature of Goddess Tripurā is explained; the creation of the universe is attributed to the union of Śiva with Śakti : the mantras that are to be used for propitiating the Goddess are given; meditation on Tripurā is presented; and there is an exposition of the different Vidyās concerning Śiva and Śakti, and of the significance of Cakras and Mudras.

(80. i, 9)

This primal Power, Goddess Tripurā, is the supreme deity. She is the great Kuṇḍalinī (residing) in the region of fire (mūlādhāra).

DEVĪ-UPANIṢAD

ATHARVA-VEDA

In this Upaniṣad, the Devī declares that she is the all; the gods pray to her with the Devī-Gāyatrī : and the Goddess is identified with Ādi-vidyā through whom sorrow is overcome.

(81. 1-3)

All the gods questioned the Devī : Who are you, O great Goddess ? She replied : I am of the nature of Brahman. From me is the world, of the nature of Prakṛti and Puruṣa, void and non-void. I am pleasure and pain. Knowledge and ignorance am I. I am the quintuplicated and non-quintuplicated elements. I am the entire world.

(81. 15)

She is the Self-Power, She entices all, holding (in her arms) a noose, a bow and an arrow. She is the great wisdom. He who knows (her) thus crosses sorrow.

BAHVṚCA-UPANIṢAD

ṚG-VEDA

In this Upaniṣad, Śakti is said to be the instrumental-cum-material cause of the world; she is described as non-dual and non-different from Brahman; and the contemplation of Śakti in different forms is prescribed.

(107. 5)

She, verily, is the self. What is different from her is unreal not-self. Hence she is Brahman-intelligence, free from the aspects of existence and non-existence. She, the consciousness which is knowledge, the non-dual Brahma-intelligence, the wave of reality, consciousness, bliss, entering what is within and what is without, shines by herself, alone. What exists as pure reality, what shines as pure consciousness, what is love and bliss—all this is the great Tripurasundarī who is of the form of all.

BHĀVANĀ-UPANIṢAD

ATHARVA-VEDA

In this Upaniṣad, the contemplation of the three-fold body as Śrī Cakra is prescribed; and the inner significance of the different acts that are done during worship is explained. The devotee is asked to imagine within himself the real meanings of these ritualistic acts and offer mental worship, e.g., service to the deity is the meditation on the reality of Brahman and the unreality of what is other than Brahman : the super-conscious state is to be regarded as prostration, etc. It is said that one who contemplates in this manner attains release.

(84. 4)

He who intensely meditates thus for three *muhūrtas* becomes released in life. He attains identity with the self of the deity. The desired ends are accomplished without effort. He alone is said to be a Śiva-Yogin.

SARASVATĪRAHASYA-UPANIṢAD

YAJUR-VEDA—TAITTIRĪYA

In this Upaniṣad, there are ten verses (Daśa ślokī) in praise of Sarasvatī : the Devī mantras are explained; the two powers of Māyā are set forth; the constituents of the universe are given; and the six kinds of Samādhi are described. The first two of the following selections are from the Daśa-ślokī.

(106. 7)

The supreme Goddess who is of the sole nature of the truth which is the purport of the Vedānta, and who becomes manifest as of the nature of name and form—may that Sarasvatī protect me.

(106. 10)

The non-dual Power of Brahman who alone is proclaimed in the four Vedas along with the auxiliary sciences and their sub-divisions—may that Sarasvatī protect me.

(106. 52-53)

Māyā has a two-fold power—of the nature of projection and of obscuration. The projective power creates the world from subtle bodies to the cosmic-egg. The other power obscures the difference between the seer and the seen within and that between Brahman and the world without. She is the cause of transmigration.

(106. 58)

Existence, manifestations, lovability, name, and form—these constitute the five-fold nature of the universe. The first three are the nature of Brahman; the other two are the nature of the world.

SĪTĀ-UPANIṢAD

ATHARVA-VEDA

In this Upaniṣad, Sītā is identified with the primal Prakṛti : and the three aspects of the Devī are explained—as will (ichchā), as activity (kriyā), and as knowledge (jñāna).

(45. 7-8)

Sitā who is to be known and who is called the primal Prakṛti becomes the support of the world because of proximity to Śrī Rāma, and also the one who creates, maintains and destroys all the embodied souls. Because of her nature as Praṇava, those who discourse on Brahman call her Prakṛti.

SAUBHĀGYALAKṢMĪ-UPANIṢAD

ṚG-VEDA

In this Upaniṣad, the Devī is described as the Goddess of Prosperity; the mantras of the Śrī Śūkta are explained as also Cakras and Mudras. There is also an exposition of two paths, yoga and jñāna, which lead to Brahman-intuition.

(105. i, 4)

Lakṣmī, the mother of all the worlds, who is seated on a clean lotus, who is of the colour of its pollen, who holds in her lotus-like hands an arrow, the symbol of fearlessness and two lotuses, who is adorned with numerous ornaments and a beautiful crown set with gems—may she be for our prosperity.